YA 537 COO

R2784

10/14

THE BASICS OF
ELECTRIC CURRENT

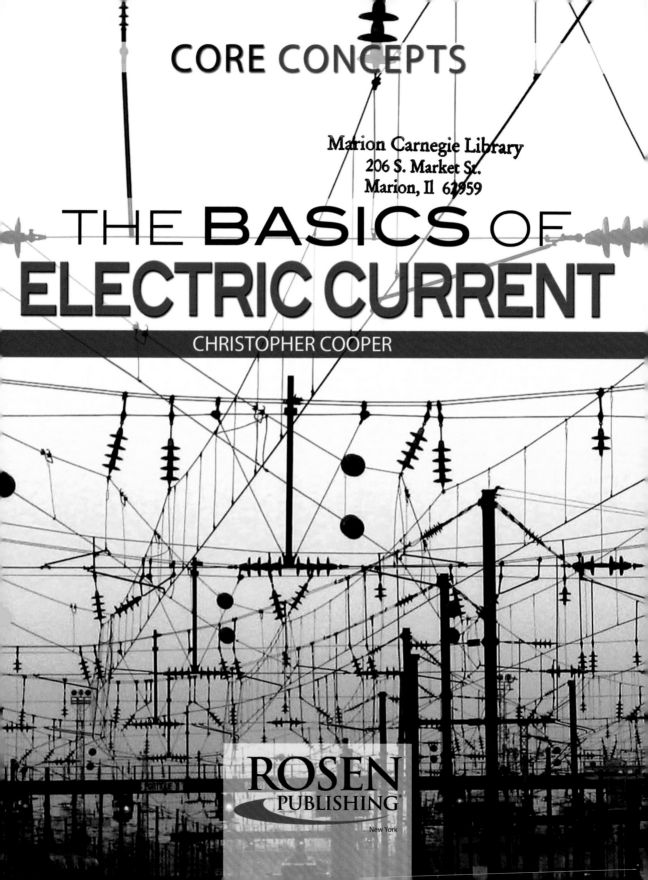

CORE CONCEPTS

THE BASICS OF
ELECTRIC CURRENT

CHRISTOPHER COOPER

ROSEN
PUBLISHING

New York

This edition published in 2015 by:

The Rosen Publishing Group, Inc.
29 East 21st Street
New York, NY 10010

Additional end matter copyright © 2015 by The Rosen Publishing Group, Inc.

Library of Congress Cataloging-in-Publication Data

Cooper, Christopher.
The basics of electric current/by Christopher Cooper.
    p. cm.—(Core concepts)
Includes bibliographic references and index.
ISBN 978-1-4777-7758-9 (library binding)
1. Electric currents—Juvenile literature. 2. Electricity—Juvenile literature. I. Cooper, Christopher (Christopher E.). II. Title.
QC527.C66 2015
537—d23

Manufactured in the United States of America

© 2004 Brown Bear Books Ltd.

CONTENTS

CHAPTER ONE

ELECTRICITY EVERYWHERE

An electric current consists of electrically charged particles in motion. Such currents produce effects that are useful to us in all kinds of ways, making electricity the workhorse of modern civilization. Electric currents can, for example, create heat, exert magnetic forces, and carry messages.

All matter is made up of electrically charged particles. Every atom has a central core, or nucleus, that contains most of its mass and is positively charged. And whirling around it are much lighter, negatively charged particles that are called electrons.

The forces between electrically charged particles are very strong. These powerful forces hold the atom together. But when equal amounts of positive and negative charge are close to each other, the effects of the charges cancel each other out, and a short distance away it is as if no charge at all were present. In normal atoms the positive charge on the nucleus is exactly balanced by the negative charge of the electrons. Electrical effects become noticeable when electrons are removed from atoms, leaving ions that have an unbalanced positive charge. (An ion is an atom or group of atoms with one or more electrons added or removed.)

When you comb your hair with a plastic comb, you sometimes see strands of hair attracted to the comb. This happens when electrons have been transferred from the comb to the hair, leaving positively charged atoms behind. The negative charges on the hair and the positive charges on the comb attract each other. This is an example of what is called static electricity.

Electric charge also shows its presence when it moves along a conductor as an electric current. When you switch on a light or a television set, electrons flow along the wires connecting the appliance to the electricity outlet in the wall and in the wires and cables connecting the outlet to the power plant. When you switch on a pocket calculator, very weak electric currents flow in the metal connections and the microchips inside the calculator.

Electric currents are important because they have so many different effects that we can use. They heat up the wires through which they flow, so they can be used in electric heaters, electric irons, and electric lamps. The currents also have magnetic effects. For example, rapidly varying electric current in a loudspeaker pulls on magnets in the loudspeaker's moving parts, which oscillate rapidly to produce sounds. Electric currents can also be used for signaling. Currents carry signals that represent sound to and from your telephone, they carry data in your computer, and they carry the information from which pictures are built up in your TV set. Electric currents made the information revolution possible.

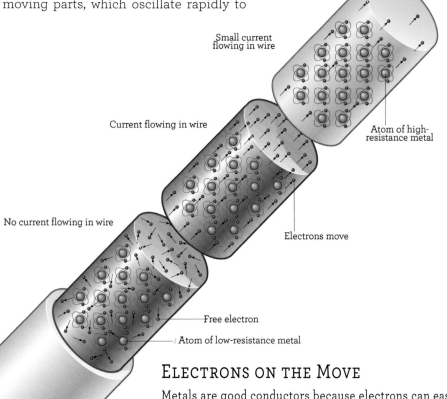

Small current flowing in wire

Current flowing in wire

No current flowing in wire

Atom of high-resistance metal

Electrons move

Free electron

Atom of low-resistance metal

ELECTRONS ON THE MOVE

Metals are good conductors because electrons can easily become detached from their atoms and form a "sea" of electrons throughout the metal wire (bottom left). When a voltage is applied along the wire (middle section) the electrons drift along together in the same direction as an electric current. If the same voltage is applied to a wire of different metal, a different current flows. If the current is smaller—that is, if fewer electrons move—the metal is described as having a higher resistance than the first one (top right). Heat is generated whenever a current flows through a conductor. The heat generated depends on the resistance of the conductor and on the amount of current flowing through it—the higher the resistance, the greater is the amount of heat.

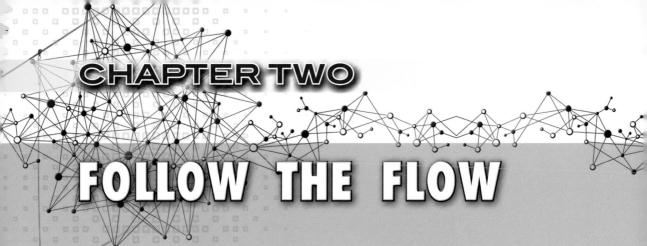

CHAPTER TWO

FOLLOW THE FLOW

Electric charges need a push to make them move. This push is called potential difference and is measured in volts. Power plants and batteries both create potential difference, on very different scales, in order to get electric currents flowing.

The physical forces you exert in combing your hair can move small amounts of charge. Pulling off an artificial-fiber shirt can have the same effect: you feel a tiny shock, and if you are in the dark, you can sometimes see sparks. When you walk on certain types of carpet, charge builds up on your body. You notice this happening when you touch a metal object, such as a faucet, and feel a small shock as the charge flows into it.

Charge flows easily through some materials, such as metals. They are called electrical conductors. It can hardly flow at all through others, such as rubber and most plastics. They are called electrical insulators. The cord to, say, a desk lamp is made of copper wires (along which the current flows) coated with plastic (through which the current cannot flow).

You will not get a shock, or see sparks, if you comb your hair with a metal comb. Electrons dislodged from your hair flow

Current flows from the high-voltage lines above the train to the locomotive's electric motors, turning shafts that drive the wheels.

away through the metal immediately and cannot build up into a sizeable quantity of charge, as they can on a plastic comb.

CREATING A CIRCUIT

An electric battery is a way of making currents flow. When the two terminals are connected through conducting wires to a device such as a flashlight bulb, an electric current is driven through the device. In chemical reactions that take place inside the battery, electrons are separated from their atoms. The electrons are forced through the wires and then through the device. When the device is disconnected the electrons cannot move, and that brings the chemical reactions to a stop—just as blocking a highway can bring traffic to a halt a long way back.

Power plants use more powerful devices for making electric currents flow. Steam, generated using the heat of burning coal, oil, or gas, or from nuclear energy, is used to drive huge turbines. Electric generators coupled to the turbines produce high-voltage current that is distributed along cables that run across a country.

In a wire in which current is flowing there are trillions of electrons in motion. But the electric charge is zero overall. The negative charge of the electrons is canceled out by the positive charge on the atoms that have lost their electrons.

VOLTAGE, RESISTANCE, AND CURRENT

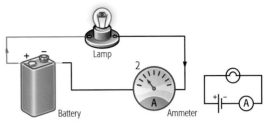

A battery and ammeter (for measuring current), both with zero resistance, are connected in series with a bulb so that the same current flows through all three. The ammeter shows that the current is 2 amps.

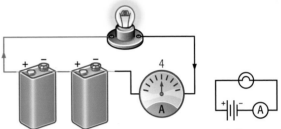

Two batteries in series give twice the potential difference across the bulb. Because the resistance in the circuit is unchanged, the current is now 4 amps.

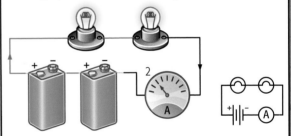

When two bulbs are connected in series their combined resistance is twice that of a single lamp. The current is halved to 2 amps.

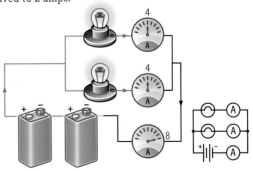

Two bulbs are connected in parallel, but each has the potential difference of two batteries across it, so a current of 4 amps again flows through each. The combined current is 8 amps.

In a newly excavated mine tunnel no power lines have yet been laid. Batteries provide the power for helmet lamps and other equipment.

If the circuit is broken, electrons immediately stop flowing. If they momentarily began to accumulate at the break or any other point in the circuit, their electric charge would repel others following behind, and instantly disperse the accumulation of charge. This is why electric current cannot flow unless there is an unbroken loop, called a circuit, that it can follow.

The "push" that drives electrons around a circuit is called potential difference, or p.d. Another name is "voltage" because p.d. is measured in volts. Ordinary flashlight batteries provide a voltage of about 1.5 volts; automobile batteries, 12 volts; and a domestic outlet for a lamp, about 110 volts (in many European countries it is 240 volts). Still higher voltages are used to send electricity across the country from the generating plants to the factories, offices, and homes where it is used.

MEASURING RESISTANCE

Most materials are neither perfect conductors nor perfect insulators. They resist the flow of current to a greater or lesser extent. A piece of wire included in a circuit to control the flow of current by its resistance is called a resistor. Resistance is measured in units called ohms. The greater the resistance of a component in a circuit, the more p.d. is needed to make a given current flow in it.

Running a plastic comb through hair may cause a small shock as electrons build up.

In a small pocket flashlight there may be a bulb with a resistance of about 3 ohms and two 1.5-volt batteries. (The total p.d. that can be delivered by a voltage source, such as a battery or generator, is called its electromotive force, or e.m.f.) The batteries are connected end-to-end so that their e.m.f.s add together to give a total voltage of about 3 volts. Current is measured in amperes, or "amps" for short. The current in amps that will flow through the bulb is given by the e.m.f. in volts divided by the resistance in ohms, in this case 1 amp. (It is actually slightly less than that because the batteries and other components in the circuit also have some resistance.)

PATH OF THE FLOW

The amount of current that will flow in a circuit depends not only on what components are connected into the circuit, but on the ways in which they are connected. In the diagram on page 9, first one and then two identical batteries are used to light a bulb. Then the two batteries are used to light two bulbs. Current-measuring

Connecting flashlights in series allows for a thin, narrow tube that also acts as the handle.

devices called ammeters are included in the circuits. The resistances of the batteries and the ammeters are so small that they can be ignored.

The bulbs are first connected in series—that is, so that the same current passes through both of them. Their resistances add, so that their combined resistance is twice the resistance of one of them. Less current flows in this case than when there is only one bulb in the circuit.

When the bulbs are connected in parallel, the current is split as it passes through them. There is the same voltage across each bulb, and it produces the same current in each bulb separately. The currents join as they flow out of the bulbs, so the combined current in the main part of the circuit is twice the current there would be if only one bulb were in the circuit. The combined resistance of the two bulbs in parallel is effectively half the resistance of each bulb singly.

Electric fences are often used to keep animals in and predators out. When an animal touches the fence and the ground at the same time, the loop is closed and electricity is allowed to flow, shocking the animal.

CHAPTER THREE

MEASURING CURRENTS

To make use of electric current it is often necessary to measure it very accurately. A device for measuring current is called an ammeter. Nearly all measuring instruments make use of the current's magnetic properties. Often it is necessary to stop the flow of current and store charge in one place, in a device called a capacitor.

Many current-measuring devices are based on the fact that an electric current sets up a magnetic field around itself. This field will move a nearby compass needle and push or pull a nearby wire carrying another current. If a wire is looped into a coil, it behaves like a magnet, with one end of the coil acting as the magnet's north pole and the other as the south pole. If such a coil is hung from a thread, and a current is passed through it, the coil will swing so that its poles are pointing north–south, just like the needle

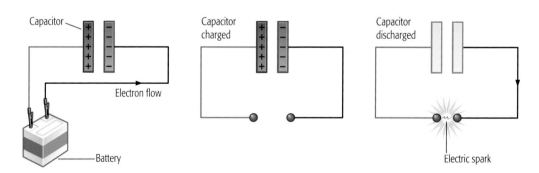

Capacitor

Electron flow

Battery

Capacitor charged

Capacitor discharged

Electric spark

CHARGING A CAPACITOR

A battery transfers electrons from one plate of a capacitor to the other. Their mutual attraction holds the electrons there when the battery is removed. The plates discharge, causing an electric spark, when the wires are brought together.

MOVING-COIL AMMETER

A current through the coil temporarily turns it into a magnet. Affected by the field of the permanent magnet, it rotates, moving the needle over a scale.

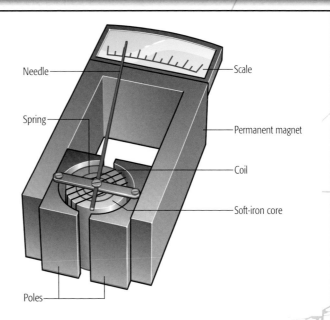

Needle

Scale

Spring

Permanent magnet

Coil

Soft-iron core

Poles

of a magnetic compass. The stronger the current flowing in the coil, the stronger the twisting force.

MOVING-COIL AMMETERS

In the usual type of ammeter, or current-measuring device, the current flows through a coil that is wound around a core of soft iron (that is, nearly pure iron, rather than steel). The core "magnifies" the coil's field. The coil is suspended between the two poles of a strong permanent horseshoe-shaped magnet. When current flows the coil twists to line up with the permanent magnet's field, but the spring by which it is suspended resists this motion. The coil turns through a greater or smaller angle, depending on the strength of the current, which is indicated by a needle attached to the moving coil and a scale.

GALVANOMETERS

A very sensitive current-measuring device, which does not use a moving needle, is called a galvanometer. Again it uses a coil suspended in the magnetic field of a permanent magnet. It is also enclosed within a draft-excluding container with a window. The coil carries a mirror, which reflects a beam of light shone in through the window. As a current flows through the coil, the coil swings backward and forward through an angle that is larger for larger currents. Several meters away the beam leaving the window forms a spot of light that moves first one way and then the other through a long distance, making very accurate measurements possible.

GALVANOMETER

The moving coil moves almost without friction in a draft-excluding chamber. It carries a mirror that reflects a light beam to a large distance, amplifying the smallest movement.

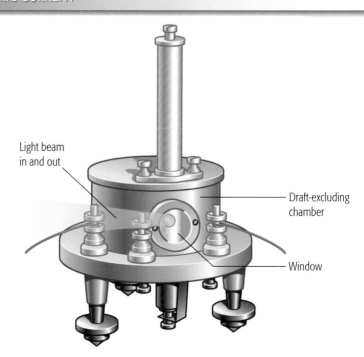

Light beam in and out

Draft-excluding chamber

Window

Galvanometers can be used in laser engraving and laser television displays.

CAPACITORS

A capacitor can store electric charge. A highly simplified type consists of two parallel metal plates (see the illustration on page 14). If they are connected to the two terminals of a battery, electrons pushed away from the negative terminal accumulate on one plate. Electrons are drawn away from the other plate by the attraction of the positive battery terminal. As electrons build up on the first plate they repel, following electrons more and more strongly, and the current falls. Electrons flowing from the second plate toward the battery are held back by the attraction of the net positive charge remaining on that plate. The current falls to zero.

If the battery is removed, and the two ends of the wires from the plates stay unconnected, the electrons stay on one plate. But if the two wire ends are brought close together, the electrons can flow across the small air-gap to the other plate, attracted by the positive charges. There is now no net charge on either plate—the capacitor has been discharged.

Capacitors are important components of electrical circuits. One type consists of two long strips of metal foil, separated by a material called a dielectric and rolled up. The dielectric increases the amount of charge that can be stored.

High-voltage capacitor banks stabilize voltage and the flow of electricity.

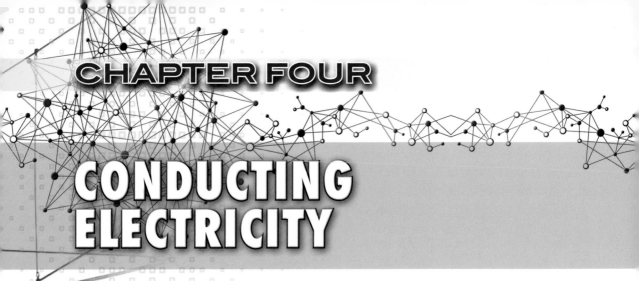

CHAPTER FOUR

CONDUCTING ELECTRICITY

The power needed to drive an electrical device, and the power that it can deliver, both depend crucially on its resistance, as well as on the voltage—that is, on the potential difference (p.d.)—applied across it. Designing an electrical device is largely a matter of putting the right amount of resistance in the right parts of its circuit.

A German physicist named Georg Ohm made an important advance in the study of electricity in the early 19th century. He found that in many materials, especially metals, the current that flows through a given piece of the material—a piece of wire, for example—is proportional to the voltage across the material. That is, if a p.d. of 10 volts is applied, twice as much current will flow as when only 5 volts is applied, provided the temperature is kept constant.

Bulbs on a Christmas tree are usually connected in groups. The members of one group are in series with one another, but the group as a whole is in parallel with other groups. When one bulb blows, all the bulbs in that group go out, but most of the bulbs keep shining.

GEORG OHM

The German physicist Georg Ohm was born in the Bavarian city of Erlangen in 1787, where he studied at the university. He published his famous law in 1827, but its importance in bringing clarity to the study of electricity, in which ideas were still very confused, was not at first recognized. He became Director of the Polytechnic Institute of Nuremberg from 1833 until 1849, and from 1852 was Professor of Experimental Physics at the University of Munich. He died in 1854. By then the value of his law, which describes the behavior of a large class of materials, had become clear. By 1870 the unit of resistance had been named in his honor.

OHM'S LAW

Ohm's law states that, provided temperature is kept constant, the ratio of the p.d. across a conductor (V) to the current flowing through it (I) is a constant, the resistance (R). This can be written in the three forms shown at the right.

$R = resistance$
$V = voltage$
$I = current$

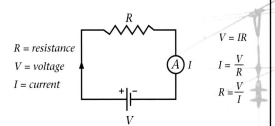

$$V = IR$$

$$I = \frac{V}{R}$$

$$R = \frac{V}{I}$$

COMBINING RESISTANCES

When resistors are connected in series, their resistances add. When they are connected in parallel, their combined resistance is less than any one of them individually, in accordance with the equation. If all the bulbs have the same resistance (far right), the current will divide as shown.

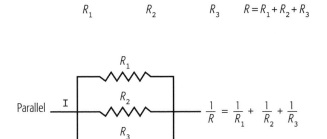

Series

R_1 R_2 R_3 $R = R_1 + R_2 + R_3$

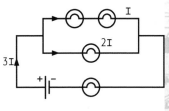

R_1

R_2

Parallel

R_3

$$\frac{1}{R} = \frac{1}{R_1} + \frac{1}{R_2} + \frac{1}{R_3}$$

No material follows this law exactly, but those that obey it approximately are sufficiently numerous to be very important and are called ohmic. The law can be written as

$$I = V/R$$

in which V is the p.d., I is the current, and R is simply the resistance of that particular piece of material. This equation can also be written in the equivalent forms

$$V = IR$$

and

$$R = V/I$$

The flow of current through a resistive material generates heat. To keep the temperature constant the heat must be continually removed. As the temperature of a material is raised, its resistance usually increases, though again, this is not true of all materials.

The resistance of a particular piece of material depends not only on what it is made of, but also on its shape. The resistance of a metal wire is much greater than the resistance of the same piece of metal melted down and formed into a shorter, fatter cylinder. For a given material, the resistance increases as length increases, and decreases as the cross-sectional area increases.

Resistors used in electrical and electronic circuits are made from metal wire or from carbon in a casing. They have their resistance marked on the casing in a code consisting of colored bands.

HOUSEHOLD METERS

Two styles of U.S. domestic electricity meter are shown here: a clock-type meter (left) and a digital meter (right). Both are registering 22,954 units (kilowatt-hours). The digital meter is becoming more widespread because it is easier to read.

ARRANGING RESISTORS

Resistors can be arranged in different ways in a circuit to produce different effective combined resistances (see the diagram on page 19). Where two or more resistors are arranged in series so that the same current flows through all of them, their resistances add up. It needs a higher p.d. to drive a given current through them.

Alternatively, resistors can be arranged in parallel so that they have the same p.d. across them, but different currents flow through them. In this case the separate currents through the different resistors combine when they emerge. The parallel resistors effectively have a smaller resistance than any one of them does by itself.

If, for example, there are three resistors, R1, R2, and R3, then the current through R1 is V/R1, and similarly for the other two. The combined current is

$$V/R1 + V/R2 + V/R3$$
or
$$V(1/R1 + 1/R2 + 1/R3)$$

This is the current that would be produced by a single resistance, R, if its value is given by the equation

$$1/R = 1/R1 + 1/R2 + 1/R3$$

So R is the combined resistance of the three resistors when connected in parallel.

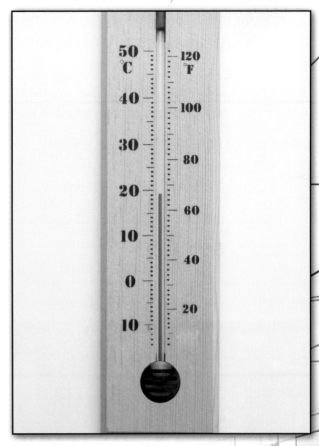

The metal mercury, once found in most thermometers, is an example of a superconductor.

CONDUCTIVE MATERIALS

All the time a current flows through a material, it generates heat. It is put to work in electric ovens, irons, toasters, kettles, and water heaters, in which current flowing through a wire makes that wire hot.

Electric lightbulbs also work on the same principle. The tungsten filaments (wires) in lightbulbs are designed to get so hot that they glow and give off light. These bulbs are described as "incandescent."

MEASURING ENERGY USED

Every electrical device requires energy to make it work. A great deal is needed by a water heater, very little by a portable radio. The rate at which energy is used by a device is called its power consumption (power is the rate of expenditure of energy). In the electrical industry power is measured in units of watts (symbol W) or kilowatts (symbol kW). A kilowatt is equal to 1,000 watts. An ordinary incandescent bulb consumes about 100 W, a toaster typically uses 1 kW, and a television set about 1/6 W. The amount of energy a device uses in a given time is found by multiplying its power consumption by the time. The unit used is the kilowatt-hour (also simply called a "unit"). It is the energy used by a 1-kW device running for 1 hour, or a 100-W device running for 10 hours.

Electricity consumers, whether in homes, offices, or factories, pay the generating companies for the amount of energy they use. A meter on the premises measures the energy used by measuring the amount of current going to the premises. The power used is the current multiplied by the voltage at which it is

Many electrical devices, including refrigerators, ovens, toasters, and blenders, are found in the kitchen of a home.

ENERGY CONSUMPTION

Here you can see the number of units of electrical energy typically used by various home appliances in 1 hour. The red circles show the energy usage in visual form.

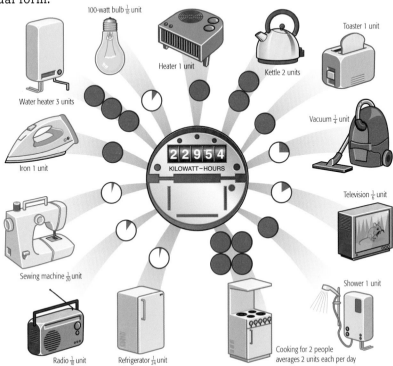

100-watt bulb $\frac{1}{10}$ unit
Heater 1 unit
Kettle 2 units
Toaster 1 unit
Water heater 3 units
Iron 1 unit
Vacuum $\frac{1}{4}$ unit
Television $\frac{1}{6}$ unit
Sewing machine $\frac{1}{20}$ unit
Shower 1 unit
Radio $\frac{1}{10}$ unit
Refrigerator $\frac{1}{24}$ unit
Cooking for 2 people averages 2 units each per day

supplied. It is continually measured and added up to give the total energy used.

SUPERCONDUCTORS

Some materials lose all their electrical resistance, becoming superconductive, when they are cooled sufficiently. This was discovered in 1911 by a Dutch physicist, Heike Kamerlingh Onnes, who found that the metal mercury becomes superconductive when its temperature is less than 4 degrees above absolute zero. Other materials show the same phenomenon at various low temperatures. From 1986 new materials were developed that show superconductivity at much higher temperatures, around 100 degrees K above absolute zero. If superconductivity at ordinary temperatures could be achieved, very cheap power transmission would become possible because very little energy would be lost from heating the transmission lines. Very fast computers could be built, and many other sophisticated new devices would become generally available.

Georg Ohm, seen here, began his career teaching mathmatics at the high-school level. He also worked as a private tutor before becoming a university professor.

This woman in South Africa is using an electrical meter. About 80 percent of people around the world have access to electricity in their homes.

CHAPTER FIVE

USING RESISTANCE

All electrical components in a circuit have some resistance, but this is not merely an inconvenience. It can be put to good use by engineers to provide us with heat and light, and to make electrical and electronic devices work in just the right way.

The heat generated when an electric current flows is caused by the current overcoming the resistance of the material through which it is flowing. The material contains imperfections and irregularities in its crystal structure, and these disturb the motion of the electrons. The more perfect a crystal is—the fewer the imperfections in its array of atoms—the less resistance it has because electrons can flow through it freely. The heating caused by a current flowing through a material with electrical resistance is called resistive heating.

The main use of resistive heating is in electric lighting. An electric bulb contains a metal filament, usually made of

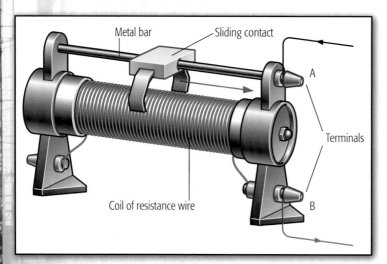

Metal bar — Sliding contact

A

Terminals

Coil of resistance wire — B

THE RHEOSTAT

Current passes from terminal A through the part of the coil of resistance wire between the contact and terminal B. As the contact is slid to the right, the current passes through less wire and hence experiences less resistance.

tungsten, which glows white-hot as current flows through it. The voltage from the power supply is (approximately) 110 volts in the United States. The power used up and converted into heat and light by a typical domestic light-bulb is 100 watts, though bulbs with power consumption ranging from 10 watts to 150 watts are available. The more power that is used, the hotter and brighter the filament becomes. The power (W) used by a bulb or any other device is equal to the current (I) that flows through it multiplied by the voltage (V) across it; in symbols,

$$W = IV$$

So a 100-watt bulb operated at 110 volts draws about 0.9 amps. The resistance of the filament needed to produce this current from this voltage is

$$R = V/I = 110/0.9$$

A tungsten filament glows white-hot as it is heated to thousands of degrees by an electric current passing through it.

which is approximately 120 ohms. A smaller resistance allows a larger current to flow, generating more power and making a brighter bulb.

A metal filament raised to the temperatures of thousands of degrees at which lightbulbs have to operate would burn up in a moment as the metal combined with oxygen in the air. That is prevented by filling the bulb with an inert (unreactive) gas such as argon or krypton. The filament lasts much longer, although it will gradually lose atoms that are driven off by the high temperature. They coat the inside of the bulb, slightly dimming it. This effect is reduced in quartz-halogen lamps, in which the bulb glass contains quartz, and the gases in the bulb include halogens such as bromine. Chemical reactions in the bulb return tungsten atoms to the filament as fast as they are lost, so the filaments have a very long life.

This is a close-up image of a tungsten filament. The filament is surrounded by inert gas to keep it from burning up too quickly.

The resistance of the various components of electrical devices must be precisely controlled in their construction in order to make the devices work properly. Some resistances must be variable. The volume control knob on traditional radio and TV sets works by increasing or decreasing the amount of resistance in the speaker circuit. The knob operates a rheostat, in which a contact slides over a coil of wire, altering the length of wire that the current flows through. The more wire the current flows through, the greater the resistance, and the current is diminished accordingly. Rheostats are also used in dimmer switches that control the lighting of a room and in instrument displays in car dashboards and bedside radios.

As this woman uses a dimmer switch to dim the lights in a room, the amount of current flowing to the lights in diminished.

CHAPTER SIX

AC AND DC CURRENTS

Once, electricity was supplied to homes and factories as one-way direct current. Now, all outlet current is AC, reversing its direction constantly. This is necessary to make power controllable, so that it can be delivered at the voltages that are needed.

The electricity that is supplied by utility companies to homes, offices, and industrial plants is not only at a much higher voltage than the electricity supplied by batteries in a portable radio or flashlight. It also differs in another crucial way. The current from a battery is direct current, or DC: it flows in one direction.

Large transformers at an electricity substation step down the voltage of the supply from the large voltages of the long-distance supply to the voltages used in factories or in homes.

DC AND AC

A battery delivers a one-way voltage that is steady. This produces a constant one-way current. It is called DC, or direct current. The graph of voltage against time is a horizontal straight line. Turbines in power plants deliver a voltage that constantly reverses in direction, creating an alternating current, or AC. The voltage–time graph then has a wavelike shape.

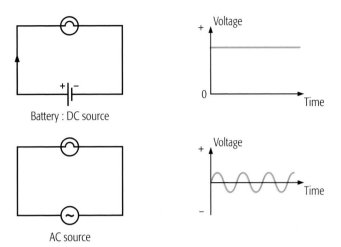

Battery : DC source

AC source

The current from the regional power grid repeatedly changes its direction. This is called alternating current, or AC.

Alternating current has immense advantages over direct current for large-scale uses. AC current has strong magnetic effects, which are vital to a host of electrical devices. And related to this is the fact that AC voltage can be altered readily, but DC voltage cannot. Different voltages are needed for different purposes. AC voltages are also easily produced by turbine generators.

USING COILS

Every electric current generates a magnetic field. If wire is looped into a coil, the whole coil behaves like a bar magnet (see chapter three). An AC current generates an alternating magnetic field.

An electric current can also be generated by a magnetic field, but only by a changing one. Moving a bar magnet near

How a Transformer Works

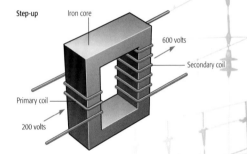

The alternating magnetic field of the primary coil is channeled through the secondary coil by the iron core. The secondary has more turns and develops a higher voltage.

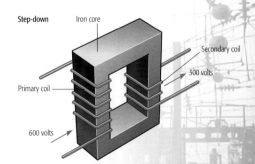

When the secondary coil has fewer turns than the primary, it develops a lower voltage, making the setup into a step-down transformer.

a wire causes a voltage to develop along the wire while the field is changing. The changing field induces a voltage. If the wire is looped into a coil of many turns, the voltage is generated across each turn of the coil, and the cumulative voltage across the whole coil is increased.

This makes it possible to alter AC voltages easily. AC current flows through a coil in one circuit, called the primary circuit. The coil is wound around an iron core, which also passes through the coil of the secondary circuit. The magnetic field generated by the primary coil creates a bigger magnetic field in the iron. This field fills the interior of the iron and passes through the secondary coil. Because the field is varying in strength and direction, it induces an AC voltage in each loop of the secondary coil. The more loops there are in the secondary coil, the bigger the voltage that develops.

If there are fewer turns in the secondary coil than in the primary coil, a smaller voltage is developed in the secondary than in the primary.

This device is called a transformer. Transformers are used to step up the voltage of current from a power station to transmit over long-distance high-voltage lines. Other transformers, housed in unmanned installations called substations, are placed near industrial plants and near residential areas to step down voltages.

AC current can be used to bring electricity to houses and buildings that are far from the closest power grid.

Nikola Tesla

CHAPTER SEVEN

STEAM MACHINES AND ALTERNATIVE ENERGY

An electricity-generating plant is a place where energy of motion is turned into electrical energy. Monster machines and huge amounts of fuel are needed. With each year that passes, the electricity-supply industry is called on to deliver more energy to the expanding industries of the world.

In a power plant turbines are spun by steam to generate electricity. The steam has to be produced by boiling purified water circulating in a closed system of pipes. Plants differ in the source of the heat they use to boil the water. Some burn coal; others, oil or gas; still others use heat from a nuclear reactor. A few use alternative forms of energy, such as sunlight or wave power, or heat from rocks deep beneath the ground.

The steam used in a conventional or nuclear power plant is superheated to temperatures of 550°C (1,000°F) or more. This steam is forced into the turbine, which consists of rotors, sets of rotating wheels equipped with fan blades, alternating with sets of fixed fan blades called stators. The steam's pressure forces the turbine's shaft to spin. The steam's temperature and pressure fall, but it is then led through lower-pressure stages of the turbine to extract as much energy as possible.

Here you can see clouds of water vapor rising above the cooling towers of a nuclear power plant.

Steam in power plants is used to power large turboalternators, such as the one seen here.

The last of the steam's heat is removed as it is circulated through pipes that are cooled by water from some external source such as a lake or river. The condensed water is returned to be heated again. The cooling water is returned to its source, though its possible effect on the environment must be carefully monitored and minimized. Warm water encourages the growth of algae, for example, which can cut down the oxygen available to fish. Clouds of water vapor can often be seen rising from the cooling towers that are a feature of many power plants.

ELECTROMOTIVE FORCE

From the steam turbine runs a shaft that spins at 3,600 rpm (in the United States) and is part of the generator. There is a strong magnetic field in the generator, which is produced by an independent supply of current flowing through electric coils called field windings. A complex structure called an armature, carrying electrical coils, spins in this magnetic field. An electromotive force of about 25,000 volts is generated.

Because the shaft rotates at 3,600 rpm, the current alternates at 60 Hz (that is, 60 hertz, or 60 times per second). This means that during 1/120 second the number of electrons flowing in one direction increases and then decreases to zero; and then during the next 1/120 second the flow builds up to a maximum in the reverse direction and then decreases to zero again. It is an alternating current (AC).

CARRYING CURRENT

The power is delivered from the generator at about 25,000 volts. It is sent to a transformer, which steps up the voltage to several hundred thousand volts. This is necessary for sending power over long distances. The electrical cables have resistance, and heat is generated in them, which is wasted. Having a very high voltage driving a low current can minimize the heat lost. The high-tension ("tension" here just means voltage) lines fan out from the plant in all directions to cities and towns in the area it serves.

These voltages are extremely dangerous, and the wires must be carried on tall towers well off the ground. They need extra support where they pass over highways. Insulators keep the current-carrying wires separated from the towers on which they are supported. In some places high-tension cables are carried in pipes buried underground.

THE SUPPLY CHAIN

A power plant converts the stored energy of its fuel into steam, which a turboalternator uses to produce a supply of electric current at tens of thousands of volts. A high proportion of the fuel's energy is inevitably lost as waste heat. Transformers boost the voltage for long-distance transmission. At substations the voltage is stepped down to supply industry and stepped down still further to supply homes and offices.

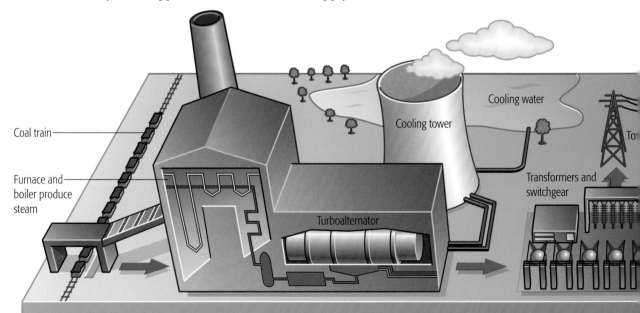

Coal train

Furnace and boiler produce steam

Turboalternator

Cooling tower

Cooling water

Transformers and switchgear

To

MICHAEL FARADAY

The discoverer of electromagnetic induction, Michael Faraday, has a host of discoveries in physics and chemistry to his name. He had attracted notice from an early age. Born the son of a blacksmith in 1791, he was largely self-educated. At the age of 21 he made notes of lectures on chemistry given by Sir Humphry Davy and showed them to Davy, who was so impressed that he gave the young man a job as his assistant. Faraday discovered new chemical compounds, including benzene; he cooled gases until they liquefied; he investigated electromagnetism—discovering the dynamo effect (page 38)— and the chemical effects of electricity. He also investigated the effects of magnetism on light. On his death in 1867 he was recognized as perhaps the greatest scientific experimenter of all time. His discovery of electromagnetic induction laid the foundations for the electricity industry that was soon to develop.

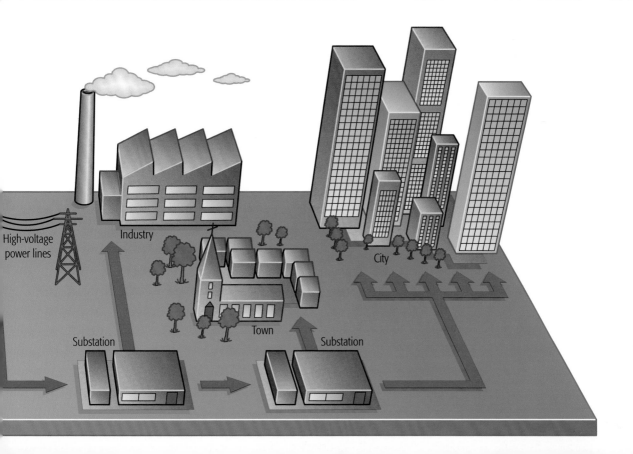

High-voltage power lines

Industry

City

Substation

Town

Substation

MOTION INTO ELECTRICITY

A dynamo can be used on a bicycle to power the lights. The turning of the wheel rotates the shaft, which generates DC current in the coils. Often the dynamo supplies a battery, which smoothes the current going to the bicycle lights.

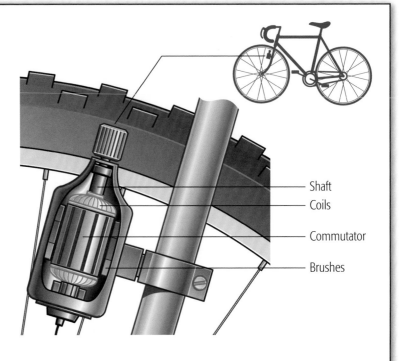

Shaft

Coils

Commutator

Brushes

SUBSTATIONS

Near an area where there are factories or other industrial plants, power cables lead to an unmanned substation. Here transformers reduce the voltages. A variety of different voltages are produced to meet the needs of different users. The substation runs automatically. It is securely fenced off because it is dangerous for any unauthorized person to wander into it.

Where power is to be delivered to homes, the voltage is finally reduced to about 110 volts (in the United States; about 240 volts in some other countries). The power is brought to an individual home along an overhead cable or under the street.

AC OR DC?

When a coil of wire rotates in a magnetic field the current in it is automatically AC. Think about what happens on one side of a single coil: the current in it alternately flows along it one way and then the opposite way because that side of the coil moves through the magnetic field one way in one half of its revolution and the other way in the other half. AC current can then be drawn from the coil by having a terminal of the external circuit that is permanently connected to each side of the coil (see illustration above).

Sometimes it is advantageous to produce DC current. In this case the connections to the generator have to be more complicated. The two terminals of the rotating coil can be in the form of the two halves of a split ring. They make contact alternately with one terminal of the external circuit and then the other (see the right-hand illustration at the top of page 27). This reverses the connection at the moment the voltage in the rotating coil reverses. The current in the external circuit is DC, though it changes in strength during each rotation of the coil.

Practical generators have to be much more complicated than this. There is a set of rotating coils, and current is drawn only from the coil that is experiencing a peak voltage at that moment. The magnetic field is provided by an electromagnet—that is, it is generated by current flowing in special coils.

FINDING OTHER SOURCES

Many people are concerned about our use of fossil fuels—coal, oil, and gas—because mining and burning them pollutes the environment, and because there are only limited reserves of them. They fear nuclear energy even more because of the problem of disposing of radioactive waste and the possibility of a serious accident that would release radioactivity into the atmosphere. They look to sunlight, the wind, waves, tides, and geothermal energy as clean and unlimited alternatives.

Large clusters of wind turbines are a common sight in the windy, low-lying regions of the Netherlands, Denmark, and other northern European countries, and there are also many in California. The electricity is generated in the wind

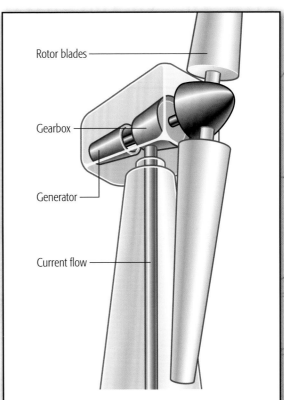

Rotor blades

Gearbox

Generator

Current flow

POWER FROM THE WIND

A wind turbine has blades shaped as carefully as the propeller or wings of an airplane to extract maximum energy from the wind. A gearbox ensures the generator is driven at the optimum speed whatever the speed of the blade. The turbine's blades may be 5 meters (about 15ft) from tip to tip. "Wind farms" of hundreds of turbines exist in some areas, including California.

turbine itself. A large machine in favorable conditions can generate around 400 kW. A very large "wind farm" generates as much power as a conventional power plant. But output is very variable, since it depends on weather conditions. Wave-power machines extract energy from the bobbing motion of sea waves.

PRACTICAL AC GENERATOR

The generators in power plants are driven by steam turbines. There is a set of rotating coils, which collectively are called the armature, and the magnetic field is provided by electric current flowing through coils called the field windings. The rings draw current from the coil in which the strongest current is flowing at that moment.

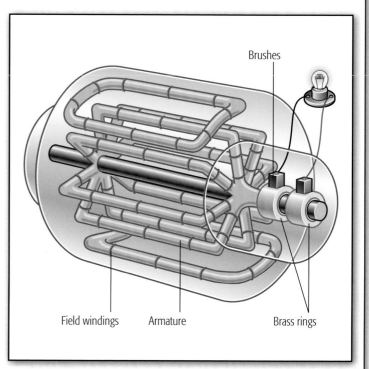

Brushes

Field windings   Armature   Brass rings

PRINCIPLE OF AC AND DC GENERATORS

In an AC generator each side of the coil is always in contact with the same terminal, so that an AC current is delivered.

In this simplified DC generator splitting-ring commutators convert the AC voltage from the rotating coil into a DC current.

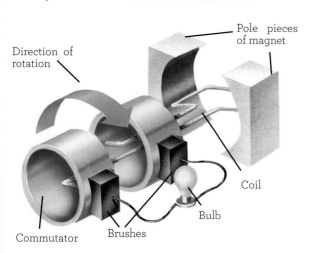

Direction of rotation

Pole pieces of magnet

Coil

Bulb

Commutator   Brushes

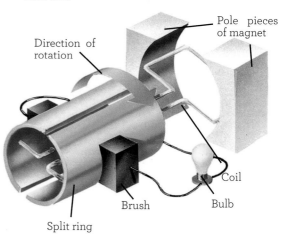

Direction of rotation

Pole pieces of magnet

Coil

Bulb

Brush

Split ring

Power plants demand an endless supply of fuel. Here a huge train of railroad cars carries coal to a generating plant.

They are located about 2 kilometers (over a mile) off the coast. The waves' motion may be used to pump air into reservoirs from which it can be released gradually to drive generators. Or it may be used to rock mechanical devices whose nodding motion is converted into electrical energy. Wave machines are unobtrusive and ideal for use wherever waves are consistently strong.

Solar energy can be turned into electricity in two ways. A large field of mirrors can be used to reflect sunlight onto a boiler, producing steam that drives a turbine in the ordinary way. Large installations in the Mojave Desert use thousands of mirrors to focus sunlight onto a vessel containing a molten salt. The salt's stored heat is used to boil water and make high-pressure steam.

The other method of converting sunlight to electricity is to allow it to shine onto a photoelectric material, which directly generates a current.

Photoelectric cells are frequently made from semiconducting materials such as silicon. On a small scale such photoelectric cells are used in solar-powered devices such as calculators. Photocells convert about 15 percent of the sunlight's energy into electrical energy. They produce DC current, which has to be converted into AC for large-scale use.

In some US states the electricity supply is deregulated. Consumers choose which energy company they will pay, and that company accordingly generates more electricity to go into the supply. The difference to the consumer is in the prices that the companies charge and also in the methods of generation they use. Some companies supply "green" electricity generated from "renewable" sources such as hydroelectricity, wind power, or solar energy, and consumers can express their preference for such sources by buying their electricity from those companies.

CHAPTER EIGHT

ELECTRICITY TODAY AND TOMORROW

Electricity is industry's workhorse in countless ways, operating switches, transmitting information, and carrying data in instruments and computers. There is a vast range of ways of generating it too, although "alternative" technology cannot yet rival the methods employed in conventional power plants.

The heat that electric currents can generate is used to good effect in many industries. High temperatures are needed to refine iron, freeing it from impurities, and in making steel by adding

This molten steel was produced in an electric furnace. Such furnaces may use AC or DC power, and large ones can produce 150 tons of steel in an hour.

controlled amounts of other materials to iron. Electric furnaces are important in this industry.

In smaller furnaces a current is passed through heating coils around the furnace. In the electric arc furnace carbon electrodes are suspended above the metal that is to be melted. A high voltage applied to each electrode in rapid succession causes an electric arc to be struck between the electrode and the metal—that is, an electric spark jumps across the gap between them, and current flows through the metal, heating it.

In the induction furnace, rapidly varying AC currents flow in coils outside the furnace. The varying magnetic field they generate penetrates the metal in the furnace and induces current in it, as in a transformer (see page 31). The current heats the metal and melts it.

Electric current has numerous other uses, not only in steelmaking but in all other industries as well. Hoists, drills, and lathes are all operated by electric motors. Electromagnetic cranes can also lift heavy loads. They contain powerful electromagnets consisting of an iron core with a current-carrying electric coil wound around it. As long as the current flows, the device is a powerful magnet capable of lifting heavy loads of metallic materials.

SOLAR VEHICLES

Scientists and engineers everywhere are working hard to exploit the potential of photoelectric cells. These cells are already indispensable in spacecraft, which can be powered for many years by sunlight, which in space is uninterrupted

This Italian solar-powered vehicle, named the Emilia 2, took part in the Australian World Solar Challenge in 2011.

Many hybrid cars are available today. Hybrid cars can be powered by both electricity and gas at different times.

and undimmed by Earth's hazy or cloudy atmosphere.

Experimental vehicles have been developed that run on solar energy alone. Many of them compete in an annual race from north to south across Australia. Winners have reached speeds of 80 kph (50 mph), but this is under exceptionally favorable conditions and with machines that are swathed in solar cells and highly streamlined.

Practical electric cars might be built, but using batteries rather than solar energy. If batteries that were more compact, lighter, and capable of storing more energy could be developed, electric cars might rival gasoline-driven cars for city use.

When the car's batteries were nearly run down, the driver would go to a resupply point—perhaps at an ordinary gas station—and exchange the old batteries for new, freshly charged ones.

The future might lie with a radical alternative to the battery called a fuel cell. It generates electricity from chemical reactions, as do batteries, but with the difference that the chemicals are supplied continuously from outside. Many types have been developed, using a variety of fuels, including hydrogen, methane, and carbon monoxide, reacting with air. Often the only waste product is water.

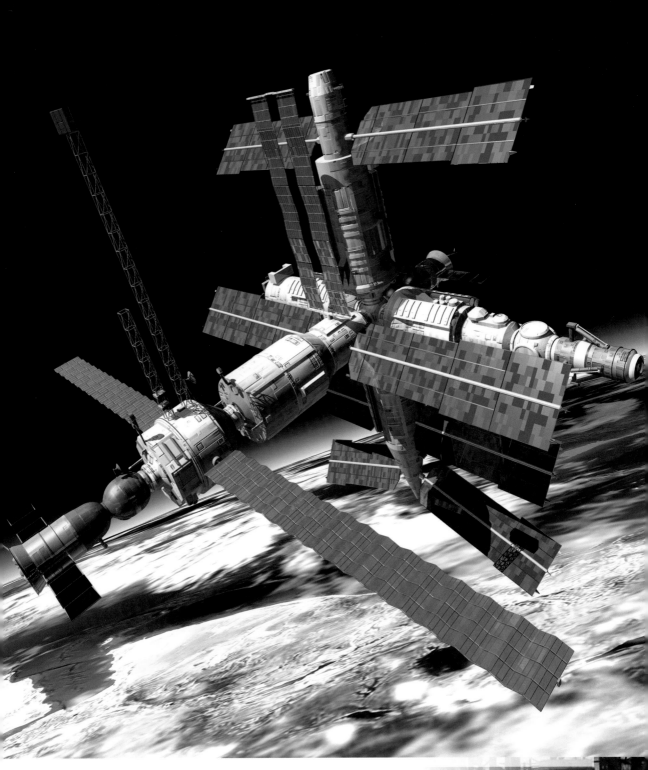

Satellites and space stations, like the one seen here, make use of solar power.

CHAPTER NINE

ELECTRICITY AROUND THE HOUSE

The ordinary person's home was revolutionized by the arrival of electricity during the 20th century. Light and warmth (or coolness) were instantly available any hour of the day or night. A host of domestic aids—washing machines, dishwashers, air conditioners, and vacuum cleaners—were made possible by electricity.

The voltage at which electricity needs to be supplied for home appliances is high enough to be dangerous. So it must be provided safely and in such a way that flaws and human error do not lead to disastrous results.

A modern American domestic supply normally delivers at least 200 amps, and possibly 440 amps or more. The electricity supply is described as being at 110 or 120 volts. Both are "nominal" values—127 volts is a typical true value, and voltage may be varied slightly at different times by supply companies. Usually a home receives a "three-wire service," via two "hot" wires and a "neutral" one. A circuit connected to one of the hot wires delivers a supply of about 120 volts; one that is connected to both delivers a supply of about 240 volts for the modern devices that require the higher voltage.

The supply is connected to the home's system through a power box, or fuse box. It contains either circuit breakers or fuses. A fuse contains a piece of wire that is designed to melt and break if too much current flows through it. A circuit breaker is a switch that automatically cuts off the current in a circuit if the current rises too high. A current surge is an indication that electricity may be dangerously leaking from some appliance. A circuit breaker can be reset when the problem has been corrected, but a "blown" fuse has to be replaced with a new one.

Inside the home, appliances are connected to the supply via two or three wires. One is called the hot or live line, while the second, along which the current returns, is called the neutral line. There is

RING CIRCUIT

The wiring to each room or floor leads from the fuse box, goes around all the power outlets, and then returns to the fuse box. An appliance that consumes a lot of power, such as a stove or water heater, has its own circuit, leading directly from the fuse box.

Meter

Fuse box

- Water heater circuit
- Ring main circuit
- Lighting
- Cooking circuit
- Power line

often a third wire, called the ground wire. It connects the casing of the device, such as a desk lamp or a TV set, to a ground wire in the household circuit that is ultimately connected, via the control box, to a metal rod sunk into the earth. If a flaw should arise, and the casing of the appliance suddenly came into contact with a high voltage, current would flow along the ground wire rather than into the body of a person touching the "live" object because of the low resistance of the ground wire and of the earth itself.

CIRCUIT WIRING

In many homes each room or floor is served by a pair of wires, called a circuit, consisting of a live wire (red) and a neutral wire (black). Lights and low-power appliances have a "single-pole" switch in the live wire only. High-power appliances use "double-pole" switches, which interrupt both wires. Each circuit leads from the fuse box, in which a common kind of fuse is the screw-in type (below).

Screw-type (plug) fuse

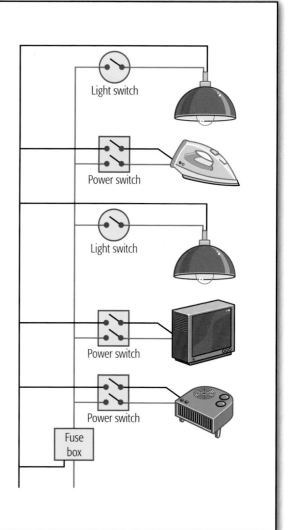

CHAPTER TEN

SENDING MESSAGES WITH WIRES

Faraday's discovery that an electric current has magnetic effects was soon applied to long-distance communication. Around 1837 the electric telegraph was invented in England and the United States. By 1900 telegraph wires girdled the Earth.

The electric telegraph was devised independently in the United States by the artist and inventor Samuel Morse, and in England by the physicist Charles Wheatstone and the engineer William Cooke. In Morse's system an operator pressed a key to allow short or long bursts of current to flow in a wire. At the other end the magnetic field of the current operated a device that made short or long marks on a roll of paper. This automatic recording system was discarded when operators found they could recognize the messages being sent from the sound of the apparatus alone. Morse developed a code in which "dots" and "dashes" (short and long pulses) represented letters and numerals.

The characters of Samuel Morse's code were designed so that the most frequently occurring letters were the shortest and quickest to send.

INTERNATIONAL MORSE CODE

Alphabet

a	b	c	d	e
f	g	h	i	j
k	l	m	n	o
p	q	r	s	t
u	v	w	x	
y	z			

Numerals

1	2	3	4
5	6	7	8
9	0		

MESSAGES ACROSS OCEANS

In 1843 Cooke and Wheatstone set up the first public telegraph line along a railroad line running westward from London. In 1844 Morse sent the message "What hath God wrought!" from Washington, D.C., to Baltimore, Maryland, along a line built with government money. Telegraph lines rapidly spread across North America and Europe, revolutionizing commerce and warfare.

The telegraph developed into the teleprinter, in which a message could be typed in on a typewriter-style keyboard and was automatically typed out at the receiver. However, the teleprinter has been superseded by e-mail and by fax. Fax (facsimile) transmission is the sending of an image of a document over telephone lines (a telephone "line" including not just wires but radio links). The document is scanned line by line, and the pattern of light and dark spots is converted into electrical pulses. At the receiver the pulses are converted back into spots for printing so that the image is reassembled on paper.

FAX MACHINE

When a fax machine transmits, the document being sent is wound through the machine, and an array of light sensors converts the image on the paper into a sequence of electronic impulses which are transmitted over an ordinary telephone line. When the machine receives, it winds heat-sensitive paper past an array of elements, each of which is briefly heated at the right moments to make dark marks on the paper. Other types of fax machine use plain paper. The keypad is used for dialing telephone numbers.

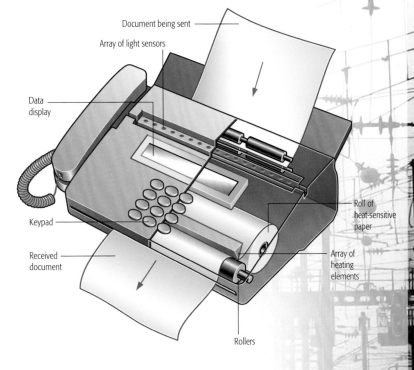

Document being sent

Array of light sensors

Data display

Keypad

Received document

Roll of heat-sensitive paper

Array of heating elements

Rollers

The giant steamship *Great Eastern* laid the first successful telegraph cable across the Atlantic in 1866. An earlier cable had failed after operating for only a short time.

Telegraph Operators

CHAPTER ELEVEN

FROM ONE TELEPHONE TO ANOTHER

Anyone who has a phone can call any other phone user in the world by pushing a sequence of buttons. The connection is made without the involvement of any other human being. Most phone calls are still carried by wires, though often with part of the connection being provided by radio links.

Modern telephone handsets work in much the same way as the first successful telephone ever built, which was made by the Scots-born American inventor Alexander Graham Bell in 1877. The sound of the speaker's voice, which consists of vibrations of the air, strikes a diaphragm, a thin piece of plastic. In one type of mouthpiece the plastic presses against a mass of carbon granules. A weak DC current supplied from the exchange passes through the carbon. As the constantly changing pressure of the air from the speaker's voice acts on the diaphragm, the diaphragm exerts a varying pressure on the granules. That affects the degree to which the granules are compressed, which in turn affects how easily an electric current can flow through the granules. The result is that a constantly varying electric current flows through the mouthpiece. In another type of mouthpiece the diaphragm moves an iron "pole piece" mounted inside a coil of wire. The moving iron causes variations in the electric current passing through the coil.

The weak varying current that emerges from the mouthpiece is an electrical copy of the pattern of sound waves that struck the mouthpiece. It travels over wires to the distant phone, where it is passed through the earpiece. It then flows through a coil forming an electromagnet. The fluctuating magnetic field that it sets up pulls on a metal diaphragm, making it vibrate in a pattern that is a copy of the original sound vibrations.

CONNECTING THE LINES

In the earliest days of the telephone a caller would first ring their local telephone exchange. An operator would then connect the caller by pushing the two ends of a wire into the two sockets corresponding to the caller and the person called.

The first automatic telephone dialing systems used a dial, which was rotated with the finger, sending a series of pulses

THE TELEPHONE NETWORK

Automatic equipment routes a phone call first to a local office, or exchange, and then through one or more long-distance offices. Finally it goes via the local office serving the person called to that person's telephone.

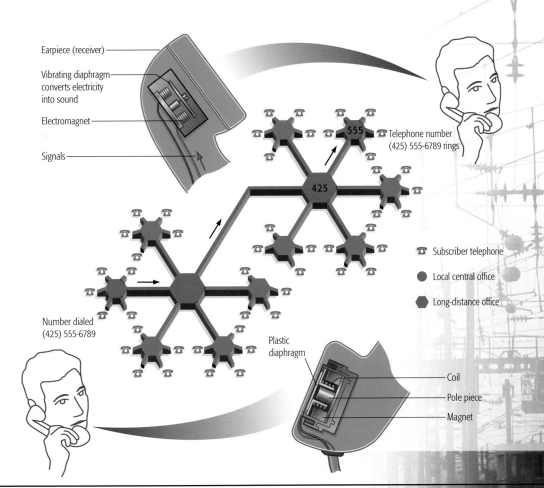

Earpiece (receiver)

Vibrating diaphragm converts electricity into sound

Electromagnet

Signals

Number dialed
(425) 555-6789

Plastic diaphragm

555

425

Telephone number
(425) 555-6789 rings

☎ Subscriber telephone

● Local central office

⬡ Long-distance office

Coil

Pole piece

Magnet

along the line. The pulses controlled the movements of a mechanical arm that rotated and moved vertically to set up the right connection. Phones are now equipped with push buttons. Pressing a button may send a series of pulses, as the old rotary dials did, or it may send audible tones that represent the numbers. The numbers that a caller dials provide an exact "route map" showing how the call must be switched to get to the right receiver.

A lineman climbs a telephone pole to carry out repairs. Electrical insulators shield the wires from the pole to prevent current from leaking down to the ground.

This early telephone operator is working the switchboard at a local telephone exchange.

CHAPTER TWELVE

CUTTING THE WIRES

The next great leap forward was to communicate at a distance without wires. Within 70 years radio communication developed from the dots and dashes of Morse code to high-quality stereophonic transmissions of voice and music.

I n the 1860s the British physicist James Clerk Maxwell predicted the existence of electromagnetic radiation—waves that consist of rapidly varying interlinked electric and magnetic fields. Movements of electric charge, he said, would cause these waves. He also said that they would travel at the speed of light. Indeed, Maxwell identified visible light, together with infrared radiation and ultraviolet radiation, as electromagnetic radiation of particular wavelengths. At that time radiations of shorter or longer wavelengths had yet to be discovered.

In 1886 some of those unknown radiations were observed. A German physicist, Heinrich Hertz, found that an electric spark sends out radiations.

WIRELESS TELEGRAPHY

Marconi made wireless transmission practical. He designed an improved oscillator, the circuit that generates high-frequency AC current. He let the AC current flow through a metal antenna, which sent out the electromagnetic radiation. He used a telegraph operator's key to generate bursts of current in the sending circuit. Marconi also improved the receiver so that it could detect signals better and amplify (strengthen) them. Eventually a loudspeaker was added.

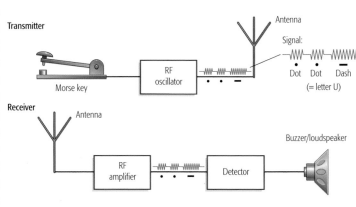

MIRRORS IN THE SKY

Radio waves of long, medium, and short wavelengths are reflected around the world from layers of ions—the ionosphere—high in the atmosphere. VHF (very high frequency) and UHF (ultrahigh frequency) waves penetrate the layers and are then relayed by artificial satellites orbiting beyond the atmosphere.

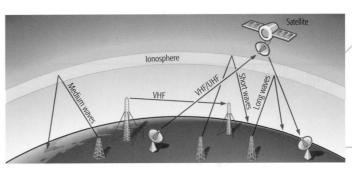

He could detect their effects with a coil of wire located some distance from the spark. The coil had a gap between its ends. As electromagnetic waves that were generated by a series of sparks passed through the coil, they induced an electromotive force—a voltage—in the coil, making sparks jump across the gap. Hertz had, in fact, sent the first radio signal. Experiments showed that the radiation traveled at the speed of light and had a wavelength much longer than that of light.

The Italian inventor Guglielmo Marconi developed radio into a practical form of "wireless telegraphy." Within six years of his first transmission he had sent signals in Morse code across the Atlantic.

Other experimenters succeeded in transmitting the sounds of voices and music by radio. In 1920 the first public radio station began regular broadcasts from Pittsburgh, Pennsylvania.

Since then, broadcasting has spread to ever-higher frequencies. Today's VHF (very high frequency) and UHF (ultrahigh frequency) broadcasts use frequencies hundreds or thousands of times higher than those of Marconi. Enormous numbers of channels can be broadcast at these high frequencies, and better signal quality can be achieved. Achieving these higher frequencies was a matter of inventing better electronic circuits to control the electric currents involved.

GUGLIELMO MARCONI

Marconi was born of an Italian father and Irish mother in 1874. He made his first experiments in wireless telegraphy in his native country, Italy, but on patenting his system in Britain, he formed the Marconi Wireless Telegraph Co. in London. In 1896 he transmitted signals over 1.5 km (1 mile); soon he had sent signals from the shore to a ship 29 km (18 miles) away. In 1899 he set up regular communication between England and France. Marconi then attempted to send radio waves from England to Canada. Most scientists assumed that radio waves must travel in straight lines and would not be able to reach places over the horizon. To their astonishment, Marconi succeeded. He shared the 1909 Nobel Prize for Physics and worked on short-wave radio for the Italian government during World War I (1914-18). He died in 1937.

CHAPTER THIRTEEN

SENDING VOICES THROUGH THE AIR

We can hear sounds from around the world whenever we want to at any time of the day or night. A microphone changes the sounds into patterns of electric currents, which are then translated into patterns of electromagnetic radiation—radio waves—that travel around the globe. The last step is to translate the electrical signals back into sounds.

The advance from sending Morse code signals to transmitting the sounds of voices or music by radio (radiotelephony) involved several major steps. Wireless telegraphy had involved sending pulses of radio waves. Radiotelephony required a continuous radio signal, called a carrier wave. Even when there is silence on a radio program, the carrier wave is being transmitted. It is a radio-frequency signal, meaning that its frequency is anywhere from very low up to 300 billion hertz (cycles per second). The wavelengths of

AM AND FM

A low-frequency sound signal can be added to a high-frequency radio carrier wave either as variations in strength (amplitude modulation, AM) or in frequency (frequency modulation, FM).

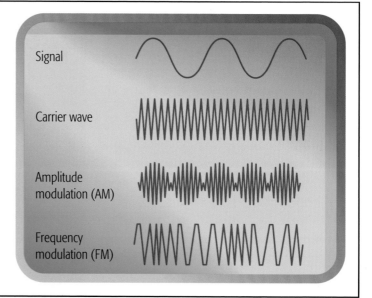

Signal

Carrier wave

Amplitude modulation (AM)

Frequency modulation (FM)

RADIO TELEPHONY

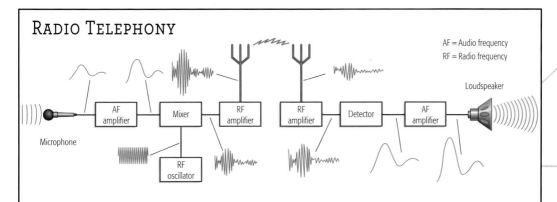

AF = Audio frequency
RF = Radio frequency

Microphone

AF amplifier

Mixer

RF amplifier

RF oscillator

RF amplifier

Detector

AF amplifier

Loudspeaker

The transmitter combines the microphone's audio-frequency signal with the oscillator's radio-frequency signal and transmits the result. The receiver picks up the RF signal, detects (extracts) the AF signal, amplifies it, and sends it to the speaker.

the radio waves vary from enormously long—up to many kilometers—down to 1 mm (1/25 of an inch).

The frequency range of sound waves is far lower—from around 20 hertz to 20 kilohertz (1 kilohertz or kHz is 1,000 hertz). The audio signal from the microphone, representing the sound waves, is combined with the carrier wave. One way of doing this is by modulating, or altering, the amplitude (strength) of the carrier wave so that it varies in exactly the same way as the microphone signal. This is called amplitude modulation (AM) and is used for LF (low- frequency or long-wave: 30–300 kilohertz, 10,000–1,000 meters) and MF (medium-frequency or medium-wave: 300–3,000 kilohertz, 1,000–100 meters) transmissions.

Another method of modulation is used for higher frequencies, which are measured in megahertz (1 megahertz = 1 million hertz). VHF, or very high frequency, is 30–300 megahertz, 1–10

meters; UHF, or ultrahigh frequency, is 10 centimeters–1 meter, 300–3,000 megahertz. Here the method of modulation is frequency modulation (FM). The amplitude of the carrier stays the same, but its frequency is varied, higher frequency representing higher amplitude of the original audio-frequency signal. Frequency is much less prone to distortion by atmospheric conditions than amplitude is, and as a result FM can give better sound quality.

VHF and UHF signals are short-range because they can penetrate the reflective layers high in the atmosphere, so they are not bent around the Earth as the lower-frequency signals are. VHF transmitters have to send their signals in tight beams along a line of sight to relay masts mounted on high ground. VHF is used by local radio stations, while lower-frequency AM signals are used for making national and international broadcasts. UHF is used for transmissions between the ground and artificial satellites, which orbit the Earth above the reflective layers in the atmosphere.

CELLULAR TELEPHONES

Cellular telephones operate with low-power radio in order that users on the same frequency in different parts of the area served do not interfere with one another. It also makes it possible to have small phones, and there is less worry about potential risks to health with lower-power phones.

The area served is divided into "cells," hence the name "cellular phone," each of which is served by one base station. It receives and transmits calls to and from the phones in its cell and the base stations of neighboring cells. Neighboring cells use different sets of frequencies so that users in the two cells do not interfere with each other. But unadjacent cells can use the same frequencies. The frequencies are in the UHF band. Cells differ in size, but are typically a few kilometers (or a few miles) across.

When a mobile phone user makes a call, the phone first transmits identification numbers to the base station, which keeps track of which phones are in its cell. The phone sends on one frequency and receives on another one, so that the two parties can both send and receive continuously, without having to switch, as with a traditional walkie-talkie or CB radio.

If the user crosses into another cell, the phone detects the weakening of the signal from the base station and requests "reregistration" in another cell. The base station arranges a "handoff" with the base station of the cell where the signal is increasing in strength. The phone switches to a new pair of frequencies provided by the new base station.

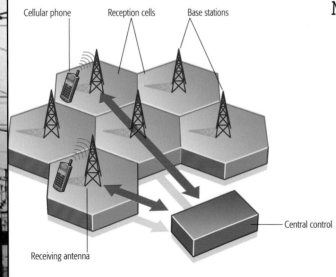

Cellular phone   Reception cells   Base stations

Central control

Receiving antenna

MOBILE PHONES

The area covered by a mobile-phone system is divided into reception cells, each served by a single base station with a receiving/transmitting antenna. Antennae in neighboring cells operate on different frequencies so that they do not interfere with each other. Sending and receiving frequencies are automatically allocated to a phone when a conversation begins. Signals travel between base stations via central control. The frequencies on which the phone operates are automatically changed if the user takes it from one cell to another.

TELLITE RELAY

Radio dish antennas on communications satellites (comsats) receive signals from the ground, amplify them, and beam them down to another ground station. The huge solar panels provide electricity for several years. Comsats relay TV, radio, and data signals around the world. They move in 24-hour orbits, 35,800 km (22,240 miles) above the equator, so they seem to remain fixed over one point on the Earth. Each receives signals from a particular ground station and sends them on to another one or to another comsat. Some Russian comsats and some military satellites have used lower orbits.

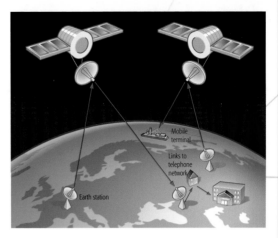

COMSATS

The enormous increase in radio, TV, phone, and computer data traffic, all demanding radio channels, has led to the use of higher and higher frequencies. These waves penetrate the reflective layers in the Earth's atmosphere, and so they are not bounced around the globe as are LF, MF, and HF (high-frequency, or shortwave) radio transmissions. They have to be relayed around the world by communications satellites, or comsats.

The great majority of comsats share a single orbit 35,800 kilometers (22,240 miles) above the equator. Here they orbit the Earth in 23 hours 56 minutes, precisely the time it takes the Earth to rotate once. A comsat has a dish-shaped receiving antenna to pick up signals from a particular Earth station. It amplifies them and sends them from another dish antenna toward another Earth station. It can also relay signals in the opposite direction between the two Earth stations.

A phone signal passing from the ground via a comsat has to travel at least

71,600 kilometers (44,500 miles), and the reply has to travel an equal distance. This introduces a time delay in conversations of at least half a second, and possibly more. New satellite systems, including the Iridium and Globalstar systems, consist of many satellites in low orbits. Being at low altitude, they can communicate directly with mobile phones, offering a vast range of new services, with no noticeable delay in conversations.

GOING DIGITAL

All aspects of telecommunications are being revolutionized as they become digital. A digital signal is one that consists of a sequence of digits (numbers).

Digital signals have several great advantages over analog signals. They give high quality. They are easily processed by computers, which work with digits. More of them can be packed into a given bandwidth (spread of frequencies). They are less vulnerable to distortion in transmission, and errors that do occur in them can be detected and corrected.

CHAPTER FOURTEEN

THE BIRTH OF TELEVISION

After radio, inventors soon found ways of sending pictures over long distances using radio waves. The result—television—has now become global in its scope, with color, stereophonic sound, and teletext. Some home television sets offer access to goods, services, and the Internet, in addition to TV programs.

Electric currents seem capable of doing anything. If they can convey sounds over immense distances, why not moving pictures seen at the same time that the events are happening? Many inventors struggled to achieve this in the 1920s and 1930s. Common to all the systems was one basic principle: A scene has to be broken down into a pattern of dots of varying brightness, a sequence of electronic signals representing these dots

Television cameras relay a baseball game to a global audience. Satellites make it possible to view events anywhere in the world on television.

TELEVISION RECEIVER

A television picture is made up of glowing dots of three colors: red, green, and blue. There is a separate beam of electrons for each color. The screen is coated with either dots or stripes of substances called phosphors, which glow the appropriate color when struck by the electron beam.

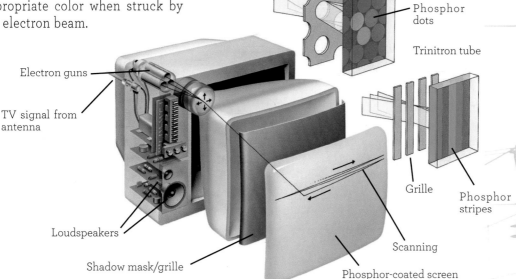

Shadow mask tube

Shadow mask

Phosphor dots

Trinitron tube

Electron guns

TV signal from antenna

Grille

Phosphor stripes

Loudspeakers

Scanning

Shadow mask/grille

Phosphor-coated screen

has to be transmitted, and the same pattern has to be reassembled on a screen in the viewer's receiver.

The first scheduled public broadcasts were made by the BBC (British Broadcasting Corporation) in 1929 using a system invented by Scotsman John Logie Baird, which used a rotating mechanical wheel in the camera and the receiver. By 1936 the BBC had abandoned Baird's system, which produced an image consisting of 240 lines, in favor of an all-electronic one with 405 lines. Electronic systems were also used in the first regular U.S. TV transmissions, which were made by NBC in 1939.

The television tube developed from the cathode-ray tube, a glass tube containing a vacuum in which an electrical terminal, the cathode, is heated so that it gives off electrons. The electrons are accelerated by a potential difference to form a cathode ray, or beam of electrons, that travels to the other end of the tube. The cathode-ray tube was invented as a scientific research tool by the British scientist William Crookes and was developed into a television device

SCANNING THE PICTURE

A TV picture consists of over a million dots of colored light arranged in 525 lines. Thirty pictures are displayed every second. Each picture is displayed in two stages. In the first stage the odd-numbered lines, 1, 3, 5, etc., are scanned. At the end of the scan the electron beam "flies back" to the beginning and scans the even-numbered lines, 2, 4, 6, etc. When the picture is complete the whole sequence begins again. This interlacing of odd and even lines reduces flicker in the image.

First scans

Second scans

Picture complete

by Boris Rozing, a Russian, and his student Vladimir Zworykin, working in the United States.

RED, BLUE, AND GREEN

In a modern television camera light from the scene is separated into red, blue, and green beams. Combinations of these three primary colors are enough to represent any color. Each beam is passed into a separate camera tube, which converts its image into a signal.

The currents from the three tubes are combined to make one signal that modulates a VHF or UHF radio wave. As a result, the signal that is broadcast contains information about the red, green, and blue parts of the scene in front of the camera, as well as an audio signal for the sound.

PICKING UP THE SIGNAL

The TV signal is picked up by the viewer's antenna, and the signal is sent into the TV set in the form of a modulated AC electric current.

In the receiver electronic circuits separate the signal into its red, green, and blue parts. They are sent to the picture tube, which is a sophisticated cathode-ray tube. Each signal controls a separate electron gun. It is a device in which a hot cathode gives off a cloud of electrons. The electrons are accelerated by electric fields so that a thin beam of electrons leaves the gun. The three electron beams go through scanning magnets, which are electric coils that bend the paths of the beams electromagnetically. The beams scan the inside of the receiver's screen from side to side and top to bottom.

The inside of the screen is coated with dots or stripes of substances called phosphors. There are three kinds on the screen: one glows red, another blue,

another green. A mask ensures that each beam reaches only the phosphor that glows the right color. When the phosphors are arranged in dots, the mask used is a shadow mask, containing accurately positioned holes. In a Trinitron screen, in which the phosphors are arranged in stripes, the mask is a grill of vertical slits. The number of electrons varies from moment to moment, separately in each beam, controlling the brightness of that color in that part of the image.

Where red and blue dots are both equally bright, magenta will be seen; red and green together make yellow; blue and

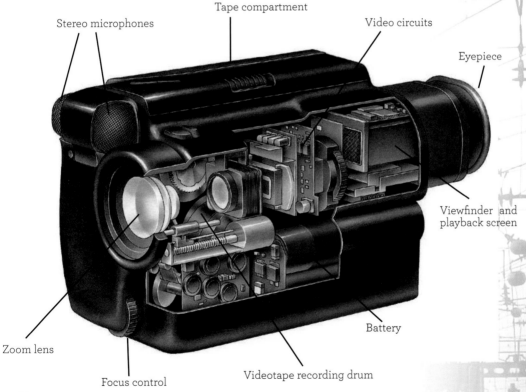

Stereo microphones

Tape compartment

Video circuits

Eyepiece

Viewfinder and playback screen

Battery

Videotape recording drum

Focus control

Zoom lens

CAMCORDER

The modern camcorder, or combined video camera and sound recorder, is a miracle of compactness. It incorporates microphones as well as a camera, and both light and sound signals are recorded onto videotape.

green make cyan. Red, blue, and green together make shades of white or gray.

Thirty different images are displayed each second (25 in some countries), but each one is scanned twice—once on the odd-numbered lines, once along the even-numbered ones—to reduce flicker. In the United States the image is made up of 525 lines; in most other countries there are 625 lines.

FUTURE OF TELEVISION

HDTV, or high-definition TV, offers a far sharper picture because it has 1,125 or more lines. It also makes a wider screen possible. These techniques call for huge amounts of information to be sent each second over the program channel. They depend crucially on computerized data compression—reducing the amount of data needed to send the information.

With interactive TV viewers can use a hand control to send signals back to the program company while viewing. They can choose different camera viewing positions during a sporting event, send opinions to a discussion program, or order goods and services from a shopping channel.

Compact portable TV sets have been developed in which the screen consists of an array of solid-state devices rather than a vacuum tube. Some use LED (light-emitting diode) displays in which each pixel (picture element) gives out light. Others use liquid-crystal displays in which each picture element allows light to pass in varying amounts according to the brightness of the picture at that point.

Older television sets that used cathode-ray tubes took up much more space than modern displays.

CHAPTER FIFTEEN

BIOGRAPHY: THOMAS ALVA EDISON

Despite his lack of formal schooling, Thomas Edison was probably the greatest inventor of all time—during his career he took out more than 1,000 patents. As much as anyone, he was responsible for creating the modern American lifestyle. Among his most successful inventions are the incandescent electric lightbulb, the movie projector, the electric typewriter, and the early gramophone or "phonograph."

When Thomas Edison was born his father was running a successful lumber business in Milan, Ohio. But the new Lake Shore Railroad, completed in 1854, bypassed Milan and brought commercial ruin to the region. The family moved to Port Huron, Michigan, where they continued to trade profitably in lumber and grain. Only in legend did Edison start life in rags; he certainly went on to acquire great riches.

Edison began school when he was eight years old but learned little there. After only three months, on hearing that a teacher had described him as "addled," his mother removed him from

Thomas Edison was often called the Wizard of Menlo Park.

KEY DATES

1847	February 11, born in Milan, Ohio
1854	Family moves to Port Huron, Michigan
1859	Edison starts work at age 12 on the newly opened Port Huron-Detroit railway as a newsboy
1863	Starts work as telegrapher
1868	Joins Western Union in Boston, Massachusetts
1869	Sets up as freelance inventor
1876	Sets up laboratory in Menlo Park, New Jersey
1878	Forms Edison Electric Light Company
1886	Moves laboratory to West Orange, New Jersey
1892	General Electric Company founded
1914–1918	Works on research projects for U.S. Navy
1931	October 21, dies at West Orange, New Jersey

school and taught him at home herself for the next few years. Thereafter, Edison, like English scientist Michael Faraday (1791–1867) before him (see page 37), was entirely self taught, learning from books and from ceaseless experimentation. Unlike Faraday, Edison had a strong business head and a drive to succeed on a wider stage.

These characteristics were immediately evident when he took his first job at age 12 as a newsboy selling papers on the new Detroit–Port Huron railroad. To supplement his earnings, he began selling fruit and candy to the passengers and soon had other boys working for him. One day he noticed an empty freight car on the train. By now, Edison had earned enough to buy a hand printing press, which he set up in the car. He wrote, printed, and sold 400 copies of his own newssheet, which he named the *Grand Trunk Herald*. There is little doubt that, if he had wanted to, Edison could have turned his abilities to creating a great retail empire. However, he was more interested in invention and in manufacturing the items he invented.

In 1863 Edison began work in the Port Huron telegraph office as an apprentice telegrapher. In comparison to modern communication methods, the electric telegraph seems a strange and very cumbersome system. Yet in its day it had an enormous impact on business and society.

This photo shows a woman working in a telegraph office. Telegraph offices quickly sprang up around the world.

ADVANCES BEFORE EDISON

The word "telegraph" simply means the transmission, or sending, of a message by signal over a distance. From earliest times, simple but urgent messages, such as warnings of invasion, were conveyed by lighting beacon fires on hilltops, or by smoke or drum signals. Toward the end of the 18th century the French engineer Claude Chappe (1763–1805) invented a way of sending more detailed messages by a system of hand-operated pivoting arms. Although the arms carried lights that allowed the signals to be used at night, such a system still required relay stations at regular distances, and could be hampered by bad weather. It was little used outside France.

The first developments in electric telegraphy began in early Victorian England. The German physicist Hans Oersted (1777–1851) had shown that an electric current flowing through a wire produces a magnetic field, which can then turn a compass needle, and in 1838 English inventor William Cooke (1806–1879) and physicist Charles Wheatstone (1802–1875) used this principle to develop the five-needle telegraph. Five magnetized needles were fixed on a panel marked with all the letters of the alphabet. When an electric impulse was sent down the wire, it deflected two of the needles to spell out a message.

MORSE CODE

The true founder of the electric telegraph industry was Samuel Morse (1791 –1872). After graduating from Yale in 1810, Morse went to England to study art. It was not until the 1830s that he became interested in electricity. Morse replaced letters with an alphabetic code in which each letter was represented by one or more dots (.), one or more dashes (-), or a combination of both. This is still known as the Morse Code. The most commonly used letters required the fewest symbols: E is indicated by a single dot, for example. The word EDISON is spelled: . (E) –.. (D) .. (I) ... (S) - - - (O) - . (N). To send the message, an operator key was depressed to complete an electric circuit. At first, the dots and dashes were embossed on a paper roll as they were received, but later a "sounding" key was developed so that a skilled operator at the other end was able to decode the message by listening to the "clicks" coming over the wire.

EDISON AND THE TELEGRAPH

The electric telegraph spread rapidly. The first line, opened in 1844, linked Washington, D.C., and Baltimore. By 1866 an underwater cable connected countries on either side of the Atlantic Ocean. The new telegraph industry created a group of young men fascinated by and skilled in the new technology, yet reluctant to settle in any one place. They moved between the main telegraph offices, demonstrating their skills and introducing new techniques and improvements.

For five years after 1863, Edison was part of this traveling community, working in Indianapolis, Cincinnati, Memphis, Boston, New York, and elsewhere. As an expert telegrapher, with a sending speed of 45 words a minute, he was never short of a job. But in 1868, Edison's hearing began to fail. It is unclear why this happened, though the condition may have started

The first telegraph message was sent between Washington, D.C., and Baltimore, Maryland, in 1844.

Modern stock tickers, such as the one seen here at the New York Stock Exchange, are electronic.

in boyhood. He never went completely deaf and was able, with some difficulty, to take part in quiet conversations. But he was forced to give up working as a telegrapher at about this time.

EARLY INVENTIONS

Edison became instead a freelance inventor. Not surprisingly, his first inventions were connected with telegraphy. Edison's Universal Stock Printer was a "stock ticker," a machine for printing out changing prices on the Stock Exchange. Western Union paid him a handsome sum for the machine. He then went on to develop the duplex, a device that doubled the capacity of a single telegraph wire by allowing operators to send messages in both directions at the same time. In 1874 he invented the quadruplex, which allowed the transmission of two messages each way. Now every mile of expensive wire was able to do the work of four miles. Railroad baron Jay Gould (1836–1892) paid Edison more than

$100,000 for the rights to this invention, despite Western Union's prior claims to it. This was to involve Edison in years of litigation. But by now his inventive mind was beginning to turn in other directions.

THE LIGHTBULB

In 1876 Edison established a laboratory and machine shop at Menlo Park, then in the rural environs of Newark, New Jersey. With two associates, Charles Batchelor, a master mechanic and draftsman, and John Kruesi, a Swiss-born machinist, he began working on a wide range of experiments. One area of investigation that took his interest was electric lighting. In 1808 the English scientist Humphry Davy (1778–1829) had connected the wires from a battery to two carbon rods and noted that "a bright spark was produced and more than half the volume of the charcoal became ignited to whiteness." This was the arc lamp. But although arc lighting replaced gas lighting in some areas, it had limited uses. The light was so bright that it was more suitable for a lighthouse than a home. It was also very hot, expensive to produce, needed regular adjustment, and smelled unpleasant.

A better option was the incandescent lamp, in which light is produced by heating a thin wire. When an electric current is passed through a filament it heats up and emits light. But whatever material was used for the filament, it completely burned away (oxidized) when mixed with oxygen in the air. The obvious answer was to enclose the filament in a glass globe from which the air had been pumped out.

One of Thomas Edison's laboratories, in West Orange, New Jersey, is now part of the Thomas Edison National Historical Park.

INVENTING FOR THE PEOPLE

The late 19th and early 20th centuries saw a flurry of inventions that would revolutionize the lives of ordinary people. More than a thousand inventions were patented by Edison himself; other groundbreaking ideas of the period included the telephone, patented in 1876 by the Scottish-born American inventor Alexander Graham Bell (1847–1922) (see page 54), and the first successful gasoline-engined automobile, built in 1885 by the German engineer Karl Friedrich Benz (1844–1929). It was vital to the success of these new products that people wanted to buy them; it was just as important, however, that they could afford them. New inventions were often expensive when first put on the market; using mass production techniques, their manufacturing costs could be reduced substantially to bring them within the reach of what most people could afford. In other words, instead of being individually handcrafted, these new commercial products were built in factories from standardized parts. Work was divided into simple, individual tasks, and specialized machinery and equipment replaced humans where possible. In 1903, the creation of a glass-blowing machine to replace human glassblowers meant that one man could now produce 1,250 lightbulbs an hour. It was this breakthrough that ensured the commercial success of Edison's incandescent lightbulb.

THE ASSEMBLY LINE

A further aid to lowering production costs was the assembly line, introduced in 1913 by American industrialist Henry Ford (1863–1947). Ford had seen the technique used in slaughterhouses, but he applied it to the production of automobiles in the Ford Motor Company plant in Detroit, Michigan. An automobile chassis was carried on a moving conveyor belt at slow speed; workers standing along the belt added parts as it passed by. In the past, one automobile had taken 12.5 hours to assemble; now it took just 1.5 hours. Using this method Ford produced his famous Model T car, known as the Tin Lizzie; by 1915 he had sold more than a million of them in the United States alone.

However, in the absence of an efficient vacuum pump, this was not an easy task. Nor was it obvious which material would make a cheap and long-lasting filament.

The first choice was carbon, the element with the highest melting point, 6,422°F (3,550°C). In 1877 Edison tested charred (carbonized) paper, but found that it burned up too quickly. Edison then turned to the metal platinum, which has a melting point of 3,222°F (1,772°C). But it failed to produce a very satisfactory light, and in any case was extremely expensive. Edison's search for a suitable filament revealed many of his great qualities: determination, persistence, ingenuity, and incredibly hard work. He often worked days and nights at a stretch, and expected his assistants to do the same. Sometimes he took brief naps on a lab bench before carrying on. In all he tested more than 1,600 materials.

Edison regarded the painstaking work as a valuable exercise: "I have not failed," he remarked on one of the tests. "I have just found 10,000 ways that won't work."

THE SOLUTION

The first real progress came when Edison heard that a much better vacuum pump had recently become available. It had been invented in 1852 by the German chemist Herman Sprengel (1834–1906). Use of the much more efficient Sprengel pump allowed Edison to consider carbon filaments again. This proved to be a messy and time-consuming business. He would start with some cotton threads, pack them with powdered carbon, heat them in a furnace, and mold them with soot. The filament would then be taken to a glass-blower who sealed it in a globe using the new vacuum pump. The filaments were drawn extremely fine, so they were very prone to breaking.

In October 1879 Edison wrote in his lab notebook that a carbon filament had worked for 13.5 hours. He added: "If I can get one to burn that number of hours, I know I can make it burn a hundred." A few days later he recorded a filament that had burned for 170 hours, and on November 1 applied for a patent for a carbon-filament lamp, and began to produce his new bulb in quantity. He later found carbonized (charred) bamboo to be better as a filament. In 1882 Edison produced 100,000 bulbs in a single year; within 20 years he was selling 45 million a year.

Improvements were gradually made to the lightbulb. The invention of a

AN EFFICIENT SYSTEM

In 1878 Edison established the Electric Light Company with the purpose of finding a safe, cheap alternative to gaslighting. To do this, he had to find a suitable circuit. If a series circuit was used, all the lights on the system would either be on or off at the same time. In this system, too, the failure of one lightbulb would cause the whole circuit to fail. Edison proposed to connect his lights in a parallel circuit by subdividing the current to run through two different wires. This could be done only by using a high-resistance system. Resistance is the opposition to the flow of current presented by the various parts of a circuit, and is measured in ohms. Current traveling through a low-resistance system generates a lot of heat, and requires thick, expensive copper cable to power an entire city district. By contrast, a high-resistance system restricts the volume of the current. It is more efficient because less current generates less heat. But a high-resistance lightbulb had not yet been invented for this system—obliging Edison to begin his search.

glass-blowing machine in 1903 meant that large quantities of lightbulbs could be produced quickly, and an inert gas such as argon was used in the bulb to avoid oxidization, thereby lengthening the life of the filament. In 1911 the carbon filament was replaced by one of tungsten, which has a melting point of 6,120°F (3,382°C). Tungsten can easily

MOVING PICTURES

By the end of the 19th century experimentation with moving photography was well under way. An early pioneer was Eadweard Muybridge (1830–1904), who succeeded in taking a series of action photographs of a trotting horse; using paper film, Frenchman Étienne-Jules Marey (1830–1903) was able to reduce exposure time to thousandths of a second to photograph insects in flight. In 1888 George Eastman (1854–1932) developed light-sensitive celluloid roll film suitable for taking moving pictures, and by 1891 William Dickson, one of Edison's employees, had built a camera, the Kinetograph, to use it, together with a device for viewing the film, called the Kinetoscope. Public viewing parlors sprang up everywhere, but the films only lasted about a minute, and they could only be viewed by one person at a time peering through a hole in a wooden box. Meanwhile the French Lumière brothers, Auguste (1862–1954) and Louis (1864–1948), had built a combined camera, printer, and projector called the Cinématographe. This projected films onto a large screen, so lots of people could view them at the same time. It had its first public demonstration in Paris on December 28, 1895, and became a huge popular success. Edison was forced to buy the rights to a film projector he called the Vitascope in order to compete with them.

be drawn into thin wires; a seven-inch length no thicker than a pencil lead can make 100 miles of filament. Tungsten also produces the familiar white electric light rather than the yellow light of the carbon filament.

ELECTRICITY'S EARLY USES

In 1882 Edison opened an electricity generating station on Pearl Street in New York City. By the close of the following year he had acquired 431 customers and was supplying power to more than 2,000 lamps. At the same time Edison and his English partner, the physicist Joseph Swan (1828–1914), opened a power station at Holborn Viaduct in London, England.

Edison's phonograph used rotating cylinders, seen here on the table. The gramophone used flat, grooved discs instead.

The age of electricity had arrived. At first the new power seemed very strange to customers used to gas; they were warned not to try to light their electric lamps with a match. However, electricity did not become common in homes for some years. By 1914 only about 10 percent of American homes had electricity, and in other countries the figure was lower. In the 19th century it was still mainly used for public lighting, gradually replacing gas lamps in streets, factories, theaters, and stores. Later it was used to power transportation; in 1903 the first electric tram service came into service in London.

Electricity was also adopted as a less brutal method of executing convicted criminals than hanging. Edison did not want the public to think of his power supply when they thought of the electric chair, so he proposed that the electricity system of his biggest rival, George Westinghouse (1846–1914), should be used. When the first execution by electricity was performed in 1890, the word "electrocution" had not been invented, and one of Edison's supporters suggested that the process should be known as being "westinghoused."

RECORDING SOUND

The name of Edison will ever be associated with the phonograph, a machine for recording sound that he began developing as early as 1877 in Menlo Park. Inventors before Edison had suggested that sounds, if they could be graphically recorded, would produce distinct shapes. Edison set out to see if he could do this. He used a carbon transmitter with a stylus tip to make indentations in a strip of paraffined paper. When the paper was pulled back beneath the stylus, he found that a vague series of sounds were generated. In other words, he had managed to record sound as graphical marks and play it back. His next model used a sheet of grooved tinfoil wrapped around a horizontal cylinder.

Edison demonstrated his phonograph ("soundwriter") in December 1877. It had

GEORGE WESTINGHOUSE 1846-1914

Like Edison, George Westinghouse was an American engineer and inventor. He learned his trade in his father's workshop, making and maintaining agricultural machinery. After serving in the Union Army during the Civil War (1861–65) and later as an engineer in the U.S. Navy, he returned home to work for his father. His first inventions were connected with the railroad. In 1865 he invented a device for getting derailed cars back onto the rails, and three years later he produced a caststeel "frog" for railroad switches (the frog is the V-shaped piece where the rails fork). In that same year, 1865, Westinghouse made his most famous invention, a brake for railroad vehicles that worked using compressed air that was generated by the locomotive. He perfected it by 1872, and within 20 years air brakes were compulsory on all trains in the United States. In 1886 he founded the Westinghouse Electric Company and championed the use of high-voltage alternating current (AC) for the distribution of electric power. His system gradually won favor over the direct-current (DC) distribution introduced by Edison, and it received nationwide acceptance after Westinghouse won the contract to build the new AC power plant at Niagara Falls on the United States–Canada border.

three main parts: a cone-shaped speaking tube, a hand-cranked cylinder covered with tinfoil, and a playback device. Speaking into the tube caused a diaphragm (a very thin disk) to vibrate. A needle connected to the diaphragm left a characteristic pattern of grooves on the foil as the crank slowly rotated it. When Edison rewound the cylinder to its original position and played it back, Edison's voice was heard emerging faintly from the tube as he recited "Mary had a little lamb...."

Improvements soon followed. An electric motor was added, a funnel amplified the sound, and wax replaced the original tinfoil. Although Edison had imagined the machine would be used by business people for dictating letters, the public had other ideas, using the phonograph almost entirely to play recorded music. However, the phonograph was soon overtaken in popularity by the superior disk gramophone, invented in 1888 by German-born American Emile Berliner (1851–1929).

FINAL YEARS

By 1886 Edison had moved from Menlo Park and set up a laboratory in West Orange, New Jersey, as a scientific research facility. There he continued to develop the phonograph and laid the foundations of the motion picture industry. He invented an alkaline storage battery that was used in submarines and designed a battery for use on Ford's Model T car. During the late 1880s and early 1890s he became involved in a disastrous magnetic ore-mining venture, which he financed using most of his General Electric Company shares. He spent the years of World War I (1914–1918) chairing a scientific advisory committee and working on ways of detecting torpedoes.

Edison carried on working well into his eighties. A huge self-publicist, ever since the 1870s he had been one of the best-known people in the world. On the announcement of his death in 1931 the lights of America were extinguished for one minute.

JOSEPH SWAN 1828–1914

Joseph Swan was born in England in the northeastern town of Sunderland. At age 14 he became an apprentice to a druggist and then worked for a manufacturing chemist. In 1871 he invented a new type of photographic plate that could be used dry instead of wet, and developed bromide paper for making photographic prints. Swan also experimented with electricity, and by 1860 had made a carbon-filament lamp. He experienced the same problems as Edison, though, and it was not until 1880 that he developed a practical lightbulb, applying for a patent while also setting up the Swan Electric Company. Swan's patent was virtually identical to Edison's. They decided to merge, setting up the Edison and Swan Joint Electric Light Company in 1883.

SCIENTIFIC BACKGROUND

Before 1850

Italian physicist Alessandro Volta (1747–1827) invents the electric battery

French engineer Claude Chappe (1763–1805) invents a hand-operated telegraph system

Samuel Morse (1791–1872) invents the Morse Code

1850

1860

1860 English chemist and physicist Joseph Swan (1828–1914) invents a carbon-filament electric lamp

1866 The first underwater telegraph cable is installed across the Atlantic Ocean between Britain and the United States

1870

1868 Edison invents an electric vote-recording machine

1876 Scots-born American inventor Alexander Graham Bell (1847–1922) patents the telephone

1877 Edison demonstrates his phonograph

1880

1879 Edison invents the electric lightbulb

1886 American engineer and inventor George Westinghouse (1846–1914) sets up the Westinghouse Electric Company

1888 American inventor George Eastman (1854–1932) develops light-sensitive celluloid roll film suitable for moving pictures

1895 The French Lumière brothers, Auguste (1862–1954) and Louis (1864–1948), mount the first public film show using their Cinématographe

1901 Italian physicist and inventor Guglielmo Marconi (1874–1937) transmits radio signals across the Atlantic

1903 The Wright Brothers, Orville (1871–1948) and Wilbur (1867–1912), make the first controlled flight in a heavier-than-air machine

1913 American industrialist Henry Ford (1863–1947) introduces the assembly line to produce his Model T car

1912 Edison produces the first talking motion pictures

1926 English physicist Edward Appleton (1892–1965) discovers the "Appleton layer" of the Earth's atmosphere, which reflects radio waves to make distant communication possible

1952 The first commercially viable video recorder is demonstrated in the United States

1982 The first compact disc players are launched by Sony in Japan

POLITICAL AND CULTURAL BACKGROUND

1851 American novelist Herman Melville (1819–1891) completes his classic tale, *Moby Dick*

1855 Alexander II (1818–1881) succeeds to the Russian throne and carries out a series of reforms, including freeing of serfs (slaves) in 1861

1861 Decades of friction over trade, slavery, and the rights of individual states lead to the outbreak of the American Civil War (1861–65)

1871 American artist James Whistler (1834–1903) completes *Arrangement in Gray and Black No. 1*, better known as "Whistler's Mother"

1876 New York's Central Park is completed after 17 years of construction

1890–91 American architect Louis Sullivan (1856–1924) designs the Wainwright Building in St. Louis, Missouri, one of the earliest skyscrapers

1898 The Spanish–American War marks the end of Spain's imperial power and leads to the fall of the Spanish monarchy three years later

1903 The Tour de France is launched by a French newspaper owner as a publicity stunt; it will become the most famous cycling race in the world

1909 American director D. W. Griffith (1875–1948) creates one of Hollywood's first stars in Mary Pickford, born Gladys Smith (1893–1979), who becomes known as "the world's sweetheart"

1920 The Government of Ireland Act divides Ireland into the six counties of the north and 26 of the south, with separate parliaments for each

1929 In the United States the Wall Street stock market crash heralds a worldwide depression; the German economy is one of many now in ruins

alternating current (AC) Electric current that flows first in one direction, then in the other, alternating many times each second. AC is used for domestic electricity supply and many other electrical applications.

alternator A generator that produces alternating current.

ammeter An instrument for measuring electric current.

ampere (A) The SI unit of electric current. A current of 1 ampere (often abbreviated to "amp") is equal to a flow of 1 coulomb per second.

anode A positive electrical terminal on a device such as a battery. Electrons flow into the device through the anode. See also *cathode*.

battery A device that generates electric current by a chemical reaction. Strictly, a battery consists of several identical units called cells, as in a car battery. However, single cells are now invariably called batteries, too.

capacitance Also called capacity, the ratio of the stored electric charge on an electrical device or other object to the voltage applied to it.

capacitor Also called a condenser, a device that stores electric charge.

cathode A negative electrical terminal on a device such as a battery. Electrons flow out of the device through the cathode. See also *anode*.

cathode ray A stream of electrons produced by the heated cathode in a vacuum tube.

cell A device that produces electricity by a chemical reaction. The word has been replaced in ordinary usage by battery.

charge A property of some subatomic particles and some larger objects that makes them exert forces on one another. Charge can be of two kinds, positive or negative.

circuit A network of electrical components that performs some function.

coil In electricity a spiral of wire through which current flows. The magnetic fields of the current in the different turns of the coil add together to make a large magnetic field; the coil is then an electromagnet.

commutator Part of a generator or motor that converts alternating current or voltage into direct current or voltage.

condenser See *capacitor*.

conductance The ability of an electrical component or other object to pass an electric current. The higher the conductance, the lower the resistance.

conductor A material or object that allows electric current to flow through it.

core A piece of iron placed in a coil to make the coil a more powerful electromagnet. When current flows in the coil, generating a magnetic field, the core becomes strongly magnetized.

coulomb (C) The SI unit of electric charge. It is equal to the charge carried by 6.24 billion electrons.

current A flow of electric charge. The current from the domestic electricity supply, from generators, and from batteries consists of a flow of electrons. Positively charged ions form part of the current inside some types of battery, moving in the opposite direction from a flow of electrons.

direct current (DC) Electric current that flows in one direction all the time, though it may vary in strength.

dynamo An electrical generator, especially one that produces direct current.

earth See *ground*.

electric field A pattern of electrical influence surrounding an electric charge or created by a varying magnetic field. At each point in space the field has a particular direction and strength.

electric potential At any point the energy derived from electric fields that a positive unit charge would gain if brought to that point from infinity. All objects tend to move in such a way as to lose energy, so positive charges tend to move from positions of high potential to positions of lower potential, while negative charges move the other way. Potential is measured in volts. See also *potential difference.*

electromagnet A device that develops a magnetic field when electric current is passed through it. It consists of a coil with a core.

electromagnetic induction The generation of an electromotive force by changes in a magnetic field.

electromagnetism The interlinked phenomena of electricity and magnetism. Every electric current generates a magnetic field. Changes in a magnetic field cause the development of e.m.f. or voltage and tend to cause current to flow.

electromotive force (e.m.f.) An electrical influence that tends to cause electric current to flow. E.m.f. is exerted by batteries and electric generators. It is measured in volts and is also called potential difference or voltage.

electron A subatomic particle, found in every atom, that carries negative charge. Most electric currents consist of electrons in motion.

electrostatic induction The movement of electric charges on an object caused by an electric field.

e.m.f. See *electromotive force.*

energy The ability of a system to bring about changes in other systems. In electricity the stored chemical energy of a battery can make electric current flow. An electrical generator uses the energy of fuel to make electric current flow.

Electric current is converted into other forms of energy where required (e.g., light in a lightbulb).

farad (F) The SI unit of capacitance. If 1 coulomb stored on an object raises the object's electric potential by 1 volt, that object has a capacitance of 1 farad. The farad is a very large unit, and the microfarad (1µF, 1 millionth of a farad) and picofarad (1 pF, 1 billionth of a farad) are commonly used.

frequency The rate at which some cyclic process repeats. The frequency of alternating current is the number of times per second that the current reaches a maximum in one direction.

fuse A piece of wire that melts (fuses) when the current passing through it becomes too large. This prevents the current from flowing, thus protecting any electrical device connected in series with the fuse.

galvanometer A sensitive device for measuring current.

generator A machine that produces an electric current. It contains coils that are rotated in a magnetic field. This generates an electromotive force in the coils by induction.

ground Also called earth, a connection to an electrical circuit into which current can flow freely. It is often a metal rod or pipe, such as a water pipe, that literally enters the ground.

hole A position in the crystal lattice of a semiconductor material at which an electron is lacking. When a neighboring electron jumps into the gap, the hole effectively moves in the opposite direction.

induction See *electrostatic induction; electromagnetic induction.*

insulator A material that is a poor conductor of electric current. Examples are rubber, many plastics, and wood. ("Insulator" is also the name given to a poor conductor of heat.) See also *conductor*.

ion An atom or molecule that has lost or gained one or more electrons so that it has an electrical charge.

joule (J) The SI unit of energy. One joule is the energy needed to move a charge of one coulomb through a potential difference of one volt.

magnetic field The pattern of magnetic influence around an object.

metal Any of a group of chemical elements in which electrons can flow easily, making them very good conductors.

motor A machine that converts energy, usually electrical energy, into motion.

ohm (Ω) The SI unit of resistance.

ohmmeter An instrument for measuring resistance.

Ohm's law At constant temperature the current through an electrical component or circuit is approximately proportional to the electromotive force across it. This relation (it is not really a "law") is enormously important despite being true only for some materials.

parallel Two electrical components in a circuit are connected in parallel if the current divides to pass through them separately. See also *series*.

photoelectric effect The ejection of electrons from a solid (especially a metal) when light falls on it.

potential difference Also called voltage, the difference in electric potential between two points. It is measured in volts. The higher the potential difference, the greater the force tending to move charges between the points.

power The rate of expending energy. The power of a motor is the rate at which it expends energy in producing motion. The power of a generator is the rate at which it produces electrical energy.

resistance A measure of how a material or a component resists the passage of electric current through it. The higher the resistance, the less current will pass when a given potential difference is applied across it.

resistor An electrical component with a known resistance, used to regulate current and voltage in a circuit.

semiconductor A material that has a resistance intermediate between that of an insulator and a conductor. In n-type semiconductors current is carried by negatively charged electrons. In p-type semiconductors current is carried by holes.

series Two electrical components in a circuit are connected in series if the same current passes through both of them in turn. See also *parallel*.

static electricity An electric charge on an object that has lost or gained electrons.

superconductivity The property of conducting electricity with no resistance at all. Some metals do this when cooled close to absolute zero (−273.15°C/−459.67°F). New complex substances have been developed that superconduct at higher temperatures (though not yet as high as 0°C).

transformer A device that increases or decreases the voltage of alternating current.

vacuum A completely empty space in which there are no atoms or molecules of any substance.

vacuum tube An airtight glass tube in which electricity is conducted by electrons passing through a partial vacuum from a cathode to an anode.

volt (V) The SI unit of potential difference.

voltage See *potential difference*.

voltmeter A device for measuring potential difference.

watt (W) The SI unit of power, equal to a rate of expending energy of 1 joule per second.

American Council on Renewable Energy
1600 K Street NW
Suite 650
Washington, DC 20006
202-393-0001
Web site: http://www.acore.org/
This nonprofit organization promotes
    the use of clean and renewable
    energy sources in the United States.
    Membership is made up of govern-
    ment officials, educators, other
    nonprofit groups, and many others.

Bakken Museum
3537 Zenith Ave South
Minneapolis, MN 55416
612-926-3878
Web site: http://www.thebakken.org/
Visitors to this museum may investigate
    how electricity is used in the human
    body and explore Frankenstein's
    Laboratory, a live show about the fic-
    tional monster brought to life with a
    jolt of electricity.

Museum of Innovation and Science
    (miSci)
15 Nott Terrace Heights
Schenectady, NY 12308
518-382-7890
Web site: http://www.schenectadymu-
    seum.org/
This museum, nicknamed miSci, fea-
    tures a planetarium, as well as many
    exhibits all about electricity and sci-
    entific innovation, including an
    exhibit on Thomas Edison and the
    lightbulb.

Museum of the Moving Image
36-01 35th Avenue
Astoria, NY 11106
718-784-0077
Web site: http://www.movingimage.us/
The Museum of the Moving Image cele-
    brates the history, artistic vision, and
    technology of film, television, and
    digital media. The core exhibition
    features over 1,400 artifacts related
    the moving images, from 19th cen-
    tury optical toys to today's video
    games.

New York Hall of Science
4701 111th Street
Corona, NY 11368
718-699-0005
Web site: http://www.nysci.org/
This hands-on museum in the borough
    of Queens opened during the 1964–
    1965 World's Fair. In 2013 the
    museum featured an exhibit on
    Nikola Tesla.

Porthcurno Telegraph Museum
Eastern House
Porthcurno, Penzance
Cornwall
TR19 6JX
United Kingdom
+44 (0) 1736 810966
Web site: http://www.porthcurno.org.uk
This museum lets visitors learn all about
    the history of the telegraph, includ-
    ing its invention, uses, and roll in
    World War II.

Spark Museum of Electrical Innovation
1312 Bay Street
Bellingham, WA 98225
360-738-3886
Web site: http://www.sparkmuseum.org/
This museum features exhibits spanning
    over 400 years of scientific discov-
    ery in the study of electricity and its
    uses. The museum also features a re-
    creation of an 18th century scientific
    laboratory.

Thomas Edison National Historical Park
211 Main Street
West Orange, NJ 07052
973-736-0550 ex. 11
Web site: http://www.nps.gov/edis/
    index.htm
At this national park, visitors can tour
    Edison's West Orange laboratory.
    Visitors can also watch early films,
    take an audio tour, and learn more
    about the Black Maria, Edison's
    film production studio, often
    called the first movie studio in
    the United States.

WEB SITES

Due to the changing nature of Internet
links, Rosen Publishing has developed
an online list of Web sites related to the
subject of this book. This site is updated
regularly. Please use this link to access
the list:

http://www.rosenlinks.com/CORE/Curr

Bureau of Naval Personnel. *Basic Electricity*. Dover Books on Electrical Engineering. Mineola, NY: Dover Publications, 2012.

Freeberg, Ernest. *The Age of Edison: Electric Light and the Invention of Modern America*. New York, Penguin Press, 2013.

Gibilisco, Stan. *Alternative Energy Demystified*. New York: McGraw-Hill Professional, 2013.

Gibilisco, Stan. *Electricity Demystified*. New York: McGraw-Hill Professional, 2012.

Gray, Charlotte. *Reluctant Genius: Alexander Graham Bell and the Passion for Invention*. New York: Arcade Publishing, 2012.

Herman, Stephen L. *Alternating Current Fundamentals*. Independence, KY: Delmar Learning, 2013.

Herman, Stephen L. *Direct Current Fundamentals*. Independence, KY: Delmar Learning, 2013.

James, Frank A. J. L. *Michael Faraday: A Very Short Introduction*. Oxford, UK: Oxford University Press, 2011.

Launey, Jean-Pierre, and Michel Verdaguer. *Electrons in Molecules: From Basic Principles to Molecular Electronics*. Oxford, UK: Oxford University Press, 2014.

McNichol, Tom. *AC/DC: The Savage Tale of the First Standards War*. San Francisco, CA: Jossey-Bass, 2014.

Parker, Steve. *Electricity*. DK Eyewitness Books. New York: DK Publishing, 2013.

Perry, Frances Melville. *Samuel Morse: Inventor of the Telegraph*. Bayside, NY: A. J. Cornell Publications, 2013.

Purcell, Edward M., and David J. Morin. *Electricity and Magnetism*. Cambridge, UK: Cambridge University Press, 2013.

Schlesinger, Henry. *The Battery: How Portable Power Sparked a Technological Revolution*. New York: Harper Perennial, 2011.

Shere, Jeremy. *Renewable: The World-Changing Power of Alternative Energy*. New York: St. Martin's Press, 2014.

Standage, Tom. *The Victorian Internet: The Remarkable Story of the Telegraph and the Nineteenth Century's On-line Pioneers*. New York: Walker & Company, 2008.

Stross, Randall E. *The Wizard of Menlo Park: How Thomas Alva Edison Invented the Modern World*. New York: Broadway Books, 2008.

Tesla, Nikola. *My Inventions: The Autobiography of Nikola Tesla*. New York: Cosimo Classics, 2011.

Zangwill, Andrew. *Modern Electrodynamics*. Cambridge, UK: Cambridge University Press, 2013.

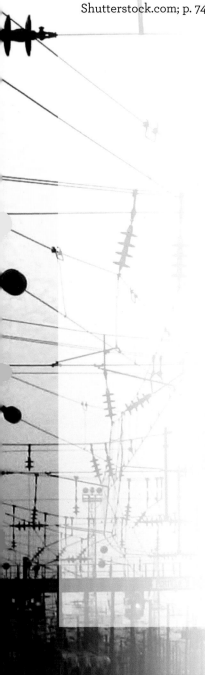

PHOTO CREDITS